Collins *gem*

Garden
Ponds

Graham Clarke

First published in 2005 by Collins, an imprint of HarperCollins*Publishers*
77–85 Fulham Palace Road, London W6 8JB
www.collins.co.uk

Based on material from the *Collins Practical Gardener* series

Created by: **Focus Publishing**, Sevenoaks, Kent
Editor: Guy Croton; Designer: Vanessa Townsend

For HarperCollins:
Senior Managing Editor: Angela Newton
Editor: Alastair Laing
Assistant Editor: Lisa John

The photographs in this book were taken by Tim Sandall, with the
exception of the images on pages 13, 20, 27, 32 and 33 that were
supplied by Hozelock Ltd.

A catalogue record for this book is available from the British Library

ISBN 0 00 720402 7

Colour reproduction by Digital Imaging
Printed and bound by Amadeus S.r.l., Italy

CONTENTS

INTRODUCTION

In the hustle and bustle of 21st century life, many consider bodies of water to be good for the soul: havens of tranquillity and serenity in a technologically manic world.

The appeal of any water feature comes down to two essential things. First, it serves up an undisputed combination of beauty and serenity. Second, all water gardeners are fascinated to discover, and to encourage, the secret hidden world that is teeming with life and interest among the depths. Yes, water gardening is as much about enjoying another 'world', as it is about looking after goldfish, installing filters and planting water irises.

Most of the plants in this book are grown for their beautiful displays of flowers and/or foliage. All of them, however, require the wet or damp conditions afforded by a pond or its edges.

A pond enhances the serenity of any garden.

HOW TO USE THIS BOOK

This book is divided into two main parts. The opening
pages guide you through the practical considerations
of gardening with aquatic plants, including planning a
water garden, planting combinations, looking after
fish and wildlife, as well as a section on pests and
diseases. The second part is an A–Z plant directory,
giving key features to help you choose the right plant.

Latin name of the
plant genus, followed
by its common name
where relevant

KEY FACTS provides
essential information on
each plant, including:

Flowers: details of flower colour
and when the plant is in flower
Plant: what is the best time of year to
plant for the best results
Site: states what sort of situation is best
for the plant in the water garden
Min Temp: gives a temperature
indication of the plant's hardiness
Height: minimum and maximum given
Spread: minimum and maximum given

CARE: The care
box gives specific
information on
additional feeding
requirements,
further details of
soil type or details
of how best to
propagate

PLANNING YOUR POND

Your garden is unique, so before you install your water feature, you should assess what features are already there, and how they might affect your plans.

If you are planning a feature that is more complex than a basic hole in the ground filled with water, then it would be wise to produce a scale drawing or plan of the area. The best way to start a paper plan is to conduct your own 'survey' of the garden. Walk around the house (and any fixed outbuildings) and make a large sketch of the layout, in plan form but not to scale.

The first thing a gardener usually wants to know when they move to a new home is in which direction the garden faces. In the northern hemisphere, a southerly facing garden gives the least amount of shade; therefore, in the southern hemisphere a northerly facing garden is the least shady.

In addition to the direction, you will need to know where the sun shines at different times of the day, and how (and

Pond pumps need ready access to a power supply.

where) the house, any outbuildings, or large trees and shrubs will cast shade. A pond should be positioned where the sun can shine upon it for at least half the day – this does not apply to very hot countries where some shade is positively beneficial.

Each garden is different, with its own specific, prevailing conditions to take into account. The illustration below is a representation of a 'typical' garden, comprising a number of different elements that usually feature in most gardens.

prevailing winds can cause problems. Do not site a pond where it will experience eddies due to winds

avoid siting a pond in the shade of a building

sunny on both sides for most of the day

a pond should be where the sun shines on it for at least half the day

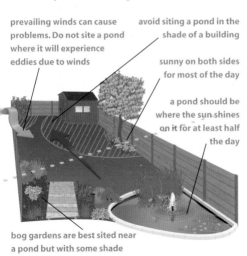

bog gardens are best sited near a pond but with some shade

POND STYLES

A small water feature could be a pebble fountain or a half-barrel with a trickling urn, both of which are ideal for a tiny town garden or patio area. Garden ponds, perhaps 1–2m (3–6ft) across, are what most gardeners would like to create, and these can be wonderful to nurture. At the top end of the scale you could opt for a lake or a large bog garden – if there is the room.

Whatever your choice of design and style for your pond, be aware that it should not be too complex, with too many niches, nooks and crannies. Always opt for the simple approach – straightforward, simple shapes are usually more attractive than awkward, complex designs.

Formal ponds need not always be this large!

Formal

Formal ponds are either circular, oval or have straight lines, in the form of a square, rectangle or some other geometric shape. They look best in more formal surroundings, such as near the house, or in conjunction with other features such as straight paths and patios.

Informal

Informal ponds work well within a small space.

By contrast, informal ponds are irregular in shape. They may have soft, sweeping curves with few, if any, straight lines or sharp angles. This type of design looks at its best in a garden planted in a relaxed way – a sort of cottage garden, with flowers of all sizes and colours. If you like lots of plants, an informal style of pond would suit you best. For example, a bog garden can be created as 'an extension' of the pond, and makes a perfect transition between pond and garden.

Fish or 'mixed' ponds

'Fish pond' is the accepted term, but perhaps 'mixed pond' would be better, for although a selection of fish may be kept in it, you would inevitably find plants and pondweed, insect life and probably amphibious life such as toads, frogs and newts in such a pond.

Regardless of the eventual constituent parts of a pond, it is the keeping of fish that many gardeners enjoy. The colours, general visual interest and serenity that fish can bring to a scene are unequalled.

Wildlife ponds

Surveys have revealed that as many as 86% of people who own a garden pond maintain that their main reason for having a pond is to 'watch and encourage wildlife'. They also agreed that informal ponds make the best environments for aquatic wildlife.

In theory, a true wildlife pond would be one that is built entirely from natural materials and contains only plants and animals native to the area. In reality,

Natural ponds are more likely to attract wildlife.

however, these preconditions are either difficult or impossible to recreate and so most wildlife ponds are artificial havens. And havens they are, for the hundreds of species that will be attracted to the pond, will themselves attract other non-aquatic animals, such as birds, bees, butterflies, hedgehogs, foxes and even badgers.

Raised ponds

Any raised feature in an otherwise flat garden will help to add interest, but one that contains water is always special. Patio ponds are often raised so that you can sit on the edge and appreciate the pond life at close quarters. It may also be the only way of having a pond if, for some reason, the ground cannot be excavated.

A raised pond can also be a disincentive to marauding creatures – predominately cats and herons, which can mercilessly decimate a collection of fish.

Graduated ponds

A sandy, muddy or stony 'beach' along one edge of a largish pond can be quite eye-catching. It will set the scene for a completely different range of plants, and will be a wonderful attraction for wildlife. Boulders, pebbles and even shells can give the effect of the foreshore. The only negative aspect is that algae might grow in the shallow water – something which rarely happens in constantly washed seawater pools.

POND MATERIALS

Ponds need to be watertight. When it comes to the material used to form the base and sides of your pond, there are three main options:
• Preformed rigid glass fibre or plastic liners
• Flexible polythene, PVC and butyl liners
• Concrete

Advantages and disadvantages

Whereas a flexible liner is the ideal solution for one gardener, another will prefer the concrete option. The following three areas will need to considered before you make your choice.

Cost

The question of comparative costs is probably the first thing you would want to investigate. However, the price of liner for a pond of a given size is very similar, whether you opt for the pre-formed type or flexible sheeting.

Ease of installation

In its simplest form, making a pond with a flexible liner involves digging a hole, placing the liner into it, and then filling it with water. Pond making could not be simpler. Yet without attention paid to trimming,

A pre-formed
rigid glass fibre
cascade.

folding,
tucking
and,
possibly,
glueing, the end
result may be
less than satisfactory.
On the other hand,
a pre-formed pond freshly
delivered from the retailer is ready
to be sunk into a hole in its chosen
place. However, the hole needs to be dug to exactly
the right shape and size, and kept perfectly level. This
is easier said than done.

Ease of maintenance

On-going maintenance is usually of concern to pond
owners who are planning to live with the same
garden for at least 10 years.

Ponds made of concrete do tend to be the most
labour-intensive in terms of on-going maintenance.
Ground movement can create cracks, and old
concrete can become brittle. Repairing kits and
sealants are expensive.

RIGID & MOULDED PLASTIC LINERS

What to look for

Rigid moulded liners made from vacuum-formed plastic are the cheapest. They are also relatively easy to install, and many people like them because the shape is predetermined.

How to buy

Garden centres usually offer a selection of pre-formed pond liners. The larger centres, or specialist aquatic and water garden retailers, can offer a better selection. There are also a number of very good mail order companies specializing in water gardening products. Wherever you choose to buy, do not simply buy the

first rigid liner you find. It will pay you to shop around until you find one that perfectly suits your requirements.

Rigid and moulded plastic pond liners.

Installing a rigid pond liner

If your chosen pond is a regular shaped unit, turn it upside down, and position it so that it is directly over where you want the finished pond to be. Mark an outline right around the rim of the unit.

If your chosen pond is kidney-shaped, for example, place it upright over its intended position and level it out with supports. Insert stakes or canes vertically into the ground at intervals around the unit.

Remove the unit, and measure the depth and size of any shelves. Dig a flat-bottomed hole to a depth that is a little deeper than the level of the first shelf. Rake over the bottom and stand the pond unit inside the hole. Press down so that the deeper section of the unit leaves an impression when removed.

Remove the unit again and excavate the newly marked section down to about 10cm (4in) below where the bottom of the pond will be. Check that the

Dig the new section below the pond's depth.

Spread a thick layer of sand on to the base.

Keep checking with
the spirit level.

Run a small amount of
water in to stabilize.

pond is sitting horizontally by using a straight-edged
board and a spirit level.

Remove any large or sharp stones. Compact the soil
and spread a 5cm (2in) layer of builder's sand on to
the base. Lower the pond gently into position; add or
take away sand until you are happy with the level.

Next, the satisfying bit – running water into the unit
for the first time. But don't fill the whole pond. Run
just a few inches into the bottom to stabilize the unit,
and to bed the bottom of it on to the sand base.

Fill in larger gaps around the edge with sieved soil or
builder's sand. Pour into the space, then ram it down
with a large piece of wood. Add more water and
backfill as you go. By filling and backfilling at the same
time, you are exerting even pressure on to the sides of
the unit, thereby preventing the walls from buckling.

Fill to about 10cm (4in) from the lip of the pond to
allow you room to plant perennials or bog plants.

FLEXIBLE UPVC LINERS

These are lengths of waterproof sheeting, enabling you to build a pond of any shape or size.

What to look for

The best reliability comes with rubber sheeting known as butyl, but PVC and LDPE (low-density polyethylene) sheets are also to be recommended.

How to buy

Most garden centres and some DIY stores offer flexible liners. Specialist aquatic and water garden retailers will offer a better selection and there are also good mail order companies specializing in water gardening products.

Installing a flexible UPVC liner

Before you dig the hole, go around the outside of the proposed site, removing a thin layer of turf or topsoil, about 45cm (18in) wide. This strip will eventually form the edge of the

Choose a liner strong enough for your needs.

Shape the sides and the shelves as you dig.

Adjust any folds as the water runs in.

pond, onto which the flexible liner will overlap, and over which the pond edging will be placed.

Then dig the rest of the hole. The sides can slope to almost any angle from a gently sloping pond to a home-made 'beach'. The shallower the slope, the better for wildlife. Shape the sides of the hole and the shelves as you dig down, allowing enough width for standing planted aquatic baskets if these are required.

If your soil is sandy or loose, install a supporting back wall – in brick or building blocks – to the top shelf to prevent damage to the edge once the pond is in use.

As excavation proceeds, keep checking with a spirit level to ensure that any shelves are horizontal. Before laying the butyl or rubber liner, install some 'underlay'. This could be a layer of builder's sand some 5cm (2in) thick, so excavate deeper to accommodate this. Pre-made underlays consist of strips of old carpet or proprietary underlay felt.

When full, trim the liner, but leave an overlap.

Cover the liner with your chosen pond edging.

Remove any sharp stones and position the underlay. If you are using sand, dampen it so that it stays in place. If you are using carpet or felt, press it down firmly. Run the underlay over any sharp corners.

The easiest way to install the liner is to mould it into the excavation, smoothing out as many creases as you can. Then run a hose into the deepest part, adjusting any folds that occur as it fills. Once the pond is full, trim the edges of the liner, leaving sufficient width all around to form a good overlap.

Before you start with your flexible liner you should always make a good estimate of the amount of liner you require. Fortunately, shortfalls can be remedied. Water pressure is usually sufficient to hold two overlapping sheets of liner in place or a thin layer of mortar can be used to 'glue' down the overlap.

Finally, cover the overlapping edge of the liner with the materials you have selected for your pond edging.

CONCRETE PONDS

Making a pond from poured concrete was once very common, but today you are more likely to come across pre-cast blocks built to form the frame of the pond, after which a flexible liner is used to hold the water.

Excavation and lining

Mark out and dig the hole, making it about 15cm (6in) deeper and wider than the desired size. Shape any shelves and firm the surface of the soil so that there are few loose fragments. Ensure that the sides are no steeper than 45 degrees – otherwise you will not be able to prevent the wet concrete from sliding to the bottom of the slope.

Concrete is a good medium for large, ornamental ponds.

Mixing and laying the base

The hole should then be lined with a 5cm (2in) thick base layer of concrete. The concrete consistency should be stiff, but moist. An hour or so after you have finished laying the base, use a stiff broom to brush the drying surface, and so create a rough key for the next layer. Leave the concrete to dry overnight.

Strengthening with wire

Next day, cover the base layer with 5cm (2in) mesh wire netting. This will reinforce the concrete. Then mix and lay another lining of concrete. Smooth the edges with a builder's trowel, and leave it to set for a couple of weeks. In really hot weather it is advisable to damp it down with a watering can.

After two weeks, spread a 5cm (2in) thick final layer of concrete over the whole area. Leave to set for a further couple of weeks.

Primers and sealants

Once the final layer of concrete has set hard, coat it with a waterproofing primer and sealant, and leave it to dry. Sweep the interior of the pond and flush out all debris prior to filling with water. This will also help initially to reduce the amount of lime in the water.

If a concrete pond has been well sealed, no toxins should leach out from the concrete. To be sure, use a pH test kit after filling the pond.

RAISED PONDS

Patio ponds are often raised so that you can sit on the edge and appreciate the pond life at close quarters.

Raised ponds need low walls to support the weight and volume of water. Good, deep foundations are crucial. A 60cm (2ft) deep trench needs to be dug, allowing for 45cm (18in) of concrete for the main foundation, and a further 15cm (6in) for the first course of bricks to remain below ground level.

Most garden walls are built with lightweight blocks. Ordinary bricks will be suitable for a small wall. Use pegs and a builder's line to mark out the position of the side of the wall that will be most visible, the 'face'.

A flexible liner is the best option. Build the outer walls of the raised pond and simply lay the liner along the bottom and up the sides. Or build another wall of

bricks or blocks to sandwich the liner in between. This gives extra durability to the liner, and always keeps it hidden.

Raised ponds are great ideas for patio areas.

CLAY-BASED PONDS

Lining a pond with compacted clay on gently sloping sides gives the impression of an entirely natural pond.

If the garden soil is unsuitable for moulding, clay may be bought in. If the existing soil is suitable, then once the hole has been dug, the base and sides must be well compacted to make it watertight. Trampling over a small area is usually sufficient. Remove all large stones and apply a layer of soot. Then line the hole with a thick, well-compacted layer of clay, building up layers to at least 15cm (6in). Plaster the clay on by hand or with a flat piece of wood. Compact it thoroughly. Once complete, add a 10cm (4in) layer of topsoil to the base, and slowly fill the pond with water, from a gently seeping hosepipe.

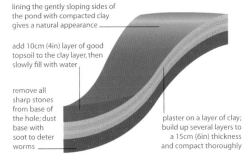

lining the gently sloping sides of the pond with compacted clay gives a natural appearance

add 10cm (4in) layer of good topsoil to the clay layer, then slowly fill with water

remove all sharp stones from base of the hole; dust base with soot to deter worms

plaster on a layer of clay; build up several layers to a 15cm (6in) thickness and compact thoroughly

ELECTRICITY & YOUR POND

Electric wiring outdoors can get damaged by cutting through a flex with a hedge trimmer or lawnmower, or digging into (and perhaps through) a buried cable.

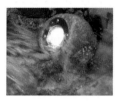

For a subtle effect, lights can be disguised as rocks.

As we know, water and electricity do not mix. From 1 January 2005 electrical installation work in England and Wales must meet the requirements of a new section of the Building Regulations, Part P. Similar regulations apply in Scotland and Northern Ireland. There is a legal requirement for you to notify your local Building Control department regarding all major electrical installations, including work outdoors, and to have such work carried out by a competent electrician. For full details, and especially if you are in any doubt about what you are able to do yourself, contact your local authority's Building Control department. See also: www.partp.co.uk; www.odpm.govluk/electricalsafety; www.scotland.govluk/build_regs; www2.dfpni.gov.uk/buildingregulations

Safety RCDs

Despite the legislation, you still need to be extremely careful when dealing with electricity in the garden. You could provide a perfect earth connection if you touch a live wire, and the short circuit that then passes through you could be fatal.

This is where residual current protection comes in. A residual current device (RCD) monitors the currents flowing in the live and neutral wires of a flex or cable and acts like a switch to cut off the electrical supply if it detects even a tiny difference (perhaps because some of the current is trying to flow through you). You will need to employ a competent person to fit an RCD for you.

Low voltage garden electric circuits

Legislation errs on the side of safety, and in many countries electrical items such as pond lights must be low-voltage: mains-voltage versions are no longer permitted.

Mains voltage garden circuits

Serious pond owners will want a permanent outside electric circuit. Basically, if you want to run power out to your garden, you have to notify the local Building Control department and get a competent person to do it for you, but once you have power outside, there are many things you can do with it, such as lighting up the rest of your garden, as well as your pond.

A normal water feature can become fabulous at night.

Lighting

Lighting can bring water alive at night, particularly during summer evenings. Interesting effects can be created by using coloured lights to illuminate water descending down a waterfall or on the upward and

downward flow of a fountain. Modestly priced kits, which often feature different coloured lights, are available from most garden centres.

A selection of external lights.

Dry ground floodlighting

Simple lighting can take the form of garden candles and torches, but a strong spotlight directed at a fountain or waterfall, causing the water droplets to sparkle against a dark background, is fairly unbeatable.

Underwater lighting creates striking effects.

Remember that you want the lighting to produce an effect – you do not want to see the source of the light. Therefore try to keep the light fittings as unobtrusive as possible (many are available in matt black for this purpose).

Aquatic lighting

Most of the true pond lights sold in kit form can be detached from the fountain nozzle and holding frame, and used instead as floating illumination. Floating spotlights can be placed beneath decking, or under a bridge, to make the structure appear to float.

Fixed underwater lighting can be directed at waterfalls for an eye-catching display. Use a high-intensity underwater light to illuminate water gushing from a vertical fountain.

PUMPS

The performance of any pump is affected by water temperature, pipe width and length, any angles in the pipework or connectors and the number of water features connected to the pump. With specific features there are such factors as the heights of fountains and falls, and the volume of water. All of these can bring about friction loss, which will affect the 'vertical head' – that is, the maximum height to which the pump can deliver water.

To calculate the right size of pump for your pond, ascertain the volume of water in your pond or feature. You will need a pump that can circulate a volume equivalent to the total volume in your pond every two hours. All good makes of pump will state on the packaging the quantity of water that they will move.

Submersible pumps

The most common type is the submersible pump, which sits within the body of water in the pond, attached to a hosepipe which carries the circulated water up and away. Submersible pumps can be relatively cheap – because of mass production – but you get what you pay for, and the cheaper models have less of a life expectancy. Never let a submersible pump run dry, as this will damage the motor.

Pumps come in many sizes and are powered accordingly.

Surface-only pumps

A pump that is designed to be used on dry land is the surface-only pump. This has the advantage of being extremely powerful, so water can be pumped over large distances or very high for a spectacular fountain display. It should be housed in a dry, well-ventilated area such as a garage or shed to avoid the problems associated with mixing electricity with water. These pumps are, however, relatively expensive. Neither do they come with many of the standard 'extras', such as connectors, strainers and hoses.

Dual purpose pump systems

This type of pump can be used as either a submersible or a surface pump. Some makes need to be housed at a lower level than the water level, so a separate tank is required. If you want to operate features such as a waterfall and fountain independently, fitting one pump for each feature will often prove more satisfactory.

FOUNTAINS

Fountains work by drawing water through a pump, then sending it through to a fountainhead or nozzle. Water is discharged in either a tumbling way or in jet-form. The optimum height for a fountain is half the width of the pond; this avoids losing water through splashing. Fountains with fine sprays generally lose more water than foaming or bubbling jets.

Jets and nozzles

The dimensions of a fountain's spray depend on the power of the pump and the flow adjuster (the device on the pump which controls the height and width of

Water jets give a pond a delightful extra dimension.

spray). For small fountains up to 1.5m (5ft) high, a low voltage pump should be sufficient.

The spray pattern is determined by the size and positions of holes in the nozzle. Single sprays are the simplest and least expensive of all fountain sprays. They suit small, unfussy ponds. Bell jet sprays emit from specially designed nozzles that produce a thin, hemispherical film of water. With this type of spray, there is very little surface disturbance when the water lands on the pond surface.

Two- and three-tiered sprays can usually be achieved by altering the design arrangement and the size of the holes in the nozzle of a single spray fountain. The more ornate the spray, however, the less desirable it becomes in an informal setting. Rotating nozzles create 'twists' of water spray; others can form double domes and columns of water.

Installation

To install a simple fountain, place a pump on an underwater platform in the centre of the pond, using a vertical discharge pipe with a fountain jet. For larger ponds where access to the pump would otherwise be a problem, it would be better to site the pump close to the edge, and use a delivery hose to connect it to the fountainhead. Extending the pond edging out and over the top of the pump can conceal it very effectively.

WATERFALLS & CASCADES

A good waterfall makes a strong statement. Sadly, it is all too easy to miscalculate waterflow, and you can readily end up with a torrent of water crashing from a wide ledge into a tiny pond; or conversely, a tiny trickle into a huge pond. Both will look anomalous.

Flow rate and 'head'

Before you install a waterfall you need a pump, but to use the right size of pump you should know the prospective height of the fall, referred to as the 'head', and the volume of water it can move (the flow rate or the amount of water flowing through the system). Manufacturer's details usually quote a flow rate for the pump and the head that the pump can produce at this flow rate.

The 'head' rate of a pump is usually adjustable.

Grotto waterfalls

This is where water falls from a fairly high header basin, directly in front of

The stepped effect of a water staircase gives a pond height.

some sort of cavern, which can be easily created with concrete. When completed and established it can be a haven for amphibious wildlife, as well as natural ferns and lichens. Alternatively, by installing the pump and outlet within the recesses of the cavern, and by raising the level of the cavern, you can create the illusion that water is coming out of the cavern and falling into the pond.

Water staircases

Classic Italian and French designers made great use of these. They would create a stone or concrete 'staircase', down which sparkling, silvery water tumbles. This feature works best if there is sufficient water flowing over it, so the size of pump should not be skimped. Disguise the ends of the steps with rocks or plants.

POND EDGING

An established pond can be a thing of beauty in a garden, but it needs an attractive surround to maximize its visual effect. A pond edging can also serve a practical purpose – such as deterring children and animals from the water's edge.

The pond surround is as important to the overall appearance of the garden as it is to the pond itself. There are many styles from which to choose. It is important for these to be planned at the same time as the pond, because otherwise the end result could be at best, incongruous, and at worst, hideous. There are three main factors to consider when edging a pond.

Decoration

Good pond edging must be decorative. This can take many forms, from paving and decking, to bog gardens and 'beaches'. Whatever style you adopt,

TIP: The least natural and most frustrating pond surround is one of maintained lawn. It is least natural because it just does not occur in the wild. It is frustrating as a pond edging because at mowing time you will not be able to avoid getting clippings onto the surface of the pond, and netting them off is a tiresome and often difficult or even dangerous activity.

there must be a degree of ornamentation. This will include planting, decorative hard landscaping or accessories (such as statues, garden lighting, bird baths, and so on).

Fence off your pond if you have small children.

Disguising pipes

Another important aspect of the pond surround is that it must hide a multitude of unsightly paraphernalia. Apart from the edges to flexible liners, the pond edging should also disguise such items as feeder and return hosepipes that come from submersible pumps, as well as any electric cables.

Safety

If young children have access to the pond, some form of barrier is advisable. These are usually fairly obvious, if unsightly. However, install a gaily painted picket-fence, or green, plastic-covered wire hoop fencing, and you overcome the problem of an unattractive appearance. Not only can such barriers stop a child from falling in the pond, they can also prevent cats and herons from getting to your fish.

CREATING A 'BEACH'

Design benefits

A graduated pond – which you may like to think of as a 'beach' – is perfect for wildlife. Do not be tempted to create the beach all the way around the pond: this will take up a huge amount of space and might look ugly.

Construction

Ponds with a beach can only really be made with flexible liners. Lay the liner as if for a normal pond; extend it from the deepest part of the pond, and slope it upwards towards the 'beach'. The liner should never be nearer to the surface than 25cm (9in). Bring the liner up against a vertical wall of soil, and trim; cover the cut ends with soil or stone. Add a 25cm (9in) depth of pebbles, shingle, sand or even mud at the

The shingle beach leads the eye into the pond.

Sandy pond beaches give the garden a seaside feel.

shallow edge, and then less depth as you work your way towards the centre of the pond.

'Muddy beaches'

This edge is best for attracting wildlife. Some way along the lined slope, build a retaining 'wall' comprising old turves, about 15cm (6in) high. Fill the area between the turf wall and the vertical part of the liner at the far end with a heavy clay loam. Compact the soil so that the far end is the same level as the adjacent garden soil or lawn. Slope the soil downwards until it meets the top of the turf wall. The water level will rise above the turf wall and be absorbed into the soil, forming the mud beach.

Sandy beaches

A sandy beach can go beyond the vertical section of liner. The sand within it will be wet, becoming drier the further you go from the pond, while the sand outside will be as damp as the surrounding soil or even bone dry in summer. Instead of a turf wall, the retaining wall should be made from mortared stone.

WOODEN DECKING

The idea of surrounding a pond with wooden decking originated in the US, Scandinavia and the Far East, but is now popular all over the world. In recent years manufacturers have emerged to make this a popular and affordable garden feature.

Design benefits

Compared with traditional paving, timber decking blends well with the garden. The decking can be constructed adjacent to the pond, ideally with enough overhang to conceal the liner. It is not a good idea for the decking to touch the pond water, as it will rot if left in prolonged contact; allow a gap of 5cm (2in) between the base of the decking and the surface of the pond at its highest level.

Entertaining/lifestyle benefits

Timber decking is consistent with the concept of the garden being a 'living space'. As a material, wood is warmer than stone paving, and more comfortable underfoot, which lends itself to barefoot traffic, especially in the warmer months. If you want to entertain regularly, it is worth having the decking (and therefore the pond) reasonably close to the house. Carefully placed trees and large shrubs can offer shade in bright sunshine, and also privacy.

Decking works well over water, but install carefully.

Decking timbers

The early forms of timber used for decking were often
untreated, and so the wood rotted or went green and
slippery. Today, pressure-treated timbers are used, and
often they are cut with many grooves along the length
of each timber to provide a key for foot traffic and so
prevent slippage in wet weather. The decking should
be constructed in accordance with good carpentry
practices, using boards and joists, and supporting
members. All pieces should be correctly jointed and
secured with galvanized fixings. Constructing the
decking from long boards is one option. Decking 'tiles'
can be very attractive, particularly in a smaller garden.

STONE PAVING

Paving can be slabs, tiles, blocks and bricks, all of which make the clearly defined pond edges. The paving style should be chosen to complement nearby hard landscaping, such as low patio walls. Manufacturers of reconstituted stone materials often design paving and walling materials that complement each other.

Design benefits

Natural and/or artificial stone can make ideal partners for a pond, whether as some kind of paving around the edge, or rock and stone to form the water feature itself. Natural quarried stone is ideal for many gardens, and sympathetic to the local environment. On the other hand, the excellent choice of artificial paving and walling (mostly concrete) can be very realistic, is cheaper, and often simpler to lay.

Construction

Paved pond edges need to be supported on well-founded low concrete or block walls. This wall can be set on top of the flexible liner, which is pulled up vertically behind the wall and concreted into place.

Lay the surface slabs flat at first. Place some of the larger stones so that they project over the water by about 5cm (2in), to cast a deep shadow line and reflection. Overhanging stones need to be large enough so that they don't topple into the water if you stand too close to the edge. If too much weight is put onto small overhanging stones, the mortar may not hold them in place.

Once you have positioned around 75% of the stones, you need to bed them down. Use a bricklayer's trowel to spread a layer of waterproof mortar about 2.5cm (1in) thick. Set each stone in position, a short distance from its neighbour. Firm or tap level with a mallet, checking all angles with a spirit level. Then fill the joints and smooth them flush with an old paintbrush.

Most importantly, when working with cement near to a pond, don't drop any into the water, or you'll have to empty and refill the pond before you introduce fish or plants.

Stone paving gives a pond a solid quality.

WATER GARDEN FEATURES

If you are short of space and do not really have room for a pond, you could consider either purchasing or building a water feature.

WATER GARDENS IN CONTAINERS

Small water features which do not require an actual pond were once rare to see; today they can be bought as manufactured items or made up at home. A small water feature can be anything from a wall-mounted ornate reservoir, through to wooden barrels, Japanese bamboo bird- and deer-scarers, and old kitchen sinks, to more sophisticated pebble and millstone fountains. These can be fairly inexpensive, quick to install and a marvellous talking point. On the downside, the small size of these features means that the range of fish or

A wooden barrel makes an ideal water feature.

plants you can keep in them is limited. Regular checks must also be made to replenish water levels.

Types of container

Pots, urns, tubs, baths, vases and water barrels really add a different dimension to the garden. Any container that can hold water is a potential above-ground pond. It should, of course, be watertight.

Siting contained water features

These containers can be placed almost anywhere in the garden, but because they are relatively small compared to a whole pond, it makes sense to site them close to where people are going to sit. The most important factor to consider is light. Do not site the water container in a dark corner; however, it should also not be positioned in full sun for the hottest part of the year or evaporation will become a problem. Another factor to consider is running power out to the container, as you will almost certainly require the water to be moved around with the aid of a pump.

TIP: Many metal, plastic or ceramic containers will already be watertight, but water barrels might be authentic old style examples made by coopers, and in these there may be gaps between the wooden slats. In this case, you should use a flexible liner to waterproof the barrel.

FOUNTAINS & WATERFALLS

Moving water is one of the joys of pond-keeping. Smaller features may include spurting frogs, millstones, lion's heads and even cherubs. Then there are the larger features requiring the movement of a greater water volume.

Fountain design

Apart from conventional spray fountains, you could opt for one of the following:

- **Wall-mounted features** These are usually cast into a block, made from concrete or reconstituted stone. A small pipe feeds water through the back and into the mouth. Water pours directly into a pool below.
- **Bubbling stones, millstones and 'boulders'** A strong steel grid holds a heavy stone fountain over an underground tank of water. A submersible pump pushes water up and through it.
- **Geyser 'foam' jets** These suck in air and mix it with the water to produce a column of foaming water.
- **'Bell' jets** These compress a flow of water from a nozzle to produce a glassy 'mushroom' of water. The pond water must be clean and free of debris.
- **Solar-powered fountains** Output is not always as good as that in conventional fountains and pumps, but it does make it possible to have a modest fountain where it would be difficult to run electricity.

Fountains, such as this millstone feature, can be small.

Waterfalls

A waterfall can be made to spill gently over a shallow sill, or gush in torrents over a high ledge, depending on its design and construction. If it is merely tipping and tumbling over rocks, then this is not a waterfall at all, but a 'cascade'. There are prefabricated, moulded units available to act as the 'header' to a waterfall. All you need to worry about is that they are level from side to side, and that the lip protrudes sufficiently over the pond, and at a suitable height, to enable a body of water to fall into the pond rather than on surrounding ground. The hosepipe linking the pump to the header pool should be carefully hidden.

PLANTS FOR YOUR POND

The attraction of a good pond is about far more than just the water. Once the pond is installed you can grow a wonderful selection of aquatic and moisture-loving plants. Aquatic and moisture-loving plants are broadly divided into the following five groups: oxygenating plants, floating aquatics, flowering aquatics, marginal plants and bog garden plants.

Oxygenating plants The reason we have pondweed, or oxygenating plants, in our ponds is because they provide oxygen. This helps to keep the water in good condition. Of all the plants we can add to our ponds, oxygenators are perhaps the least interesting, yet almost certainly the most important. By day, oxygenators convert dissolved carbon dioxide, given off by the fish, into oxygen. They also consume minerals and nutrients that otherwise would be used by troublesome algae.

Myriophyllum aquaticum is a good oxygenator.

Most oxygenators will grow rapidly and can cause the pond to become congested. Hook out a few bucketsful of excess 'weed' two or three times during the summer period. This will, curiously, make the weed grow faster, and in turn make it more efficient at filtering and conditioning the water.

Eichhornia crassipes is a common floating aquatic.

Floating aquatics Floating water plants are not anchored by roots, although some do produce a few straggly roots that just dangle in the water.

Aquatic plants such as waterlilies – with roots which are firmly anchored – are discussed in the 'flowering aquatics' section. There are, however, plenty of free-floaters, with no discernible rooting or anchorage, such as water hyacinth (Eichhornia), duckweed (Lemna) and water chestnut.

'Floaters' help to maintain clear water; by blocking out some of the sunlight, they effectively check the development of algae. As with oxygenators, they also offer refuge for small aquatic creatures, which can hide in the warmer waters beneath the surface.

Some floating plants increase their size and number rapidly and, as with the oxygenators, can cause overcrowding. There is a restriction in the sale of such plants in some warmer climates.

Flowering aquatics The distinction between 'flowering aquatics' and 'marginals' is somewhat blurred. Flowering aquatics can be grown in the margins of a pond and in this case it will be in the section covering 'marginals'. Plants covered here are more at home in the centre of the pond. Flowering aquatics grow within the pond, anchored in the mud or in planting containers.

Flowering aquatic plants generally produce leaves and flowers that sit on top of the water or rise above it. Waterlilies are the classic flowering water plant, and they typify one of the most important aspects of the group, in that the vigour of their surface spread, and the depth of water to which they are most suited means they must be chosen with great care.

Pontaderia cordata is a good flowering aquatic plant.

Marginal plants

Although there are arguments over the true definition of a 'marginal' plant, in reality a 'marginal' should be considered to be any plant that grows at the very edge of the water, regardless of the moisture content of the soil in which it is growing. This means that the marginal plants

Lobelia cardinalis is an excellent marginal plant.

discussed later will have a wide range of habitat requirements, spanning all soil conditions from being permanently under water to semi-dry.

Bog garden plants At one end of the bog plant list are those species that like practically to be in the water, and are therefore just slightly removed from the marginals. At the other end there are those plants that require merely a consistently moist soil.

Bog garden plants – also known as marsh or poolside plants – generally dislike dry, clay soil that can turn concrete-like in hot, dry weather. Also, they tend not to perform well if they are exposed to high winds and full sun all day long. Other than that, they

Myosotis palustris 'Alba'
(bog garden plant)

enjoy a wide and varied selection of growing conditions.

Many have colourful flowers and lush, attractive foliage, and they make the perfect transition between pond and garden (as long as the soil is moist).

Grasses and ferns Both are grown for their foliage, as a foil for other plants and as an attraction in their own right. There are dozens of species that are perfectly at home either in the pond itself (true aquatics) or in the moist conditions of the bog garden.

Ornamental grasses Thanks to gardening trends, these have become fashionable. There is a bewildering array of species and varieties to choose from, such as the architectural pampas grass and the clump forming smaller forms, like Festuca.

Grass-like plants are perfect for growing in and around a pond. Their slender stems form elegant, vertical clumps that make an ideal contrast to the bold lines of formal ponds, as well as blending and contrasting with other plants in an informal pond.

Festuca glauca 'Golden Toupee' (ornamental grass)

Although some members of the grass family grow in the water (rushes and sedges), most of the smaller ornamental species prefer a moist but free-draining soil.

Ferns These shade-loving plants are perfect for the waterside, with their delicate, fresh green leaves (more correctly, 'fronds'). Few plants suggest the prehistoric quite like the fern. They have been around since the age of the dinosaur, which means that they are sturdy, durable and hardy. More often than not they grow in damp places although, it has to be said, a dank atmosphere is as important to them as a wet soil. Indeed, it is quite a common occurrence for the crown and roots of outdoor ferns to rot in consistently wet soil.

Matteuccia struthiopteris is a good fern for the waterside.

CHOOSING & BUYING PLANTS

Mid-spring to early summer are the best times to plant up a pond and most garden centres will be stocking a wide range of aquatic and moisture-loving plants during this period. Specialist water garden nurseries tend to offer better quality plants. The prices can vary, too, with specialist centres often selling plants at as much as half the price you would pay at a general garden centre. Also, specialist aquatic nurseries can provide customers with good, informed advice; not all general centres can provide this.

Inspect plants thoroughly before buying.

Spring and early summer are the best times to plant because the pond water will be sufficiently warm to provide a receptive environment for new plants. You can usually buy aquatic plants up until late summer or even autumn, however.

Plants are sold either bare-rooted or grown in containers. The former will be sold in plastic

Oxygenating plants are often displayed and sold in tubs.

bags for planting as soon as you get home. The latter can be left in their containers until you are ready to plant them – but do not let them dry out. Keep them submerged in a tray of water or in the pond itself.

Recognizing healthy plants

There are certain things you should look out for. Plants you are considering for purchase should look fresh and healthy with plenty of new growth: avoid any with a lot of dead leaves that could have already spread disease through the entire plant.

Take a good look at the display. Marginal and deep-water aquatics are usually displayed in trays of water, which should be reasonably clean. The soil into which aquatic plants are planted must be consistently moist, so avoid any which have been allowed to dry out.

Plants should be clearly labelled, but do not buy any with badly faded labels – a clear indicator that they have been sitting around for a long time.

Nurseries should stock clearly labelled plants.

Mail order

If you are not happy with your local source of aquatic plants, it is worth considering placing an order with a specialist mail order supplier. You will often find choice and even rare plants with these companies, and many of the plants will have been propagated and grown by them as well.

Modern packaging and reasonable postage costs mean that the plants generally arrive in good condition. It usually compares favourably when you work out the cost of driving to a garden centre and then paying what can sometimes be inflated prices.

The downside to mail order is that you cannot see the plants before you buy them, so it is important to use only companies with a good reputation, or which offer a full money-back guarantee for peace of mind.

Before you plant

Once you have got the plants home, you should plant them straight away. If planting is delayed, keep the plant continually moist. Ideally, oxygenators and deep-water plants should be submerged in pondwater or rainwater. They can survive in this state for two to three weeks, after which time their condition will begin to deteriorate.

Waterlilies, in particular, benefit from a little preparation before planting. If any roots are damaged, or are excessively long, use a sharp knife or pair of secateurs to cut them back to within 5cm (2in) of the tuber. Remove any leaves that have unfurled close to the base, being careful not to damage any new growth. Do not interfere with any young, tightly rolled leaves that are still growing; they will soon reach the water surface.

TIPS:
- Do allow new ponds to stabilize before planting
- Do not be tempted to buy poor quality plants
- Do rinse bare root aquatic plants before you plant or pot them
- Do not collect plants from the wild

INSTALLING PLANTS

Before plastics were commonly used, most pond plants were set directly into the mud in the bottom of the pond. This is ideal for a large wildlife pond where the planting is, for the most part, left to its own devices.

If you want to do this with your own pond, place a layer of soil about 15cm (6in) deep onto the base of the pond liner. Plant directly into this soil and then fill the pond very slowly – over a week or more – to avoid stirring up the soil.

Soils

Special aquatic composts can be purchased, although ordinary garden soil (sifted to remove twigs, roots and stones) is perfectly acceptable. Use a heavy loam, such as the fertile top layer taken from your pond

Line the container with hessian cloth.

Put a layer of soil in the base of the container.

Carefully position the plant in the soil.

Add a layer of gravel to just below the rim.

excavation. Do not add peat, as this will float out into the pond, and do not incorporate garden compost or manure to the soil.

Planting in mesh containers

Aquatic plants are best planted in hessian cloth inside plastic mesh containers. Planted containers can be positioned in the pond at any desired point, and they can easily be moved when cleaning or maintenance is necessary.

The planting procedure is straightforward. Line the plastic mesh container with hessian (sack) cloth. Put a layer of soil in the hessian at the base of the container [B], and then position the plant in it, ensuring that its existing soil level is just below the rim. Fill with soil to within 2.5cm (1in) of the top of the container and gently firm the soil. Add a layer of fine gravel to just below the rim of the pot. This stops soil floating out of the pot, prevents fish from nosing around and stirring up the soil, and provides an attractive finish. Then water the container thoroughly.

Setting out the plants

Marginal plants can be placed directly in their final positions. Deep water aquatics – plants that need a depth of at least 20cm (8in) to grow well – need to be 'acclimatized' gradually to their eventual planting position and level. Do this by placing the planted container on a base of bricks – one to four bricks deep, depending on the desired depth. The plants' foliage at this planting stage should be just below the surface of the water. Place some padding under the brick so that the liner does not become damaged. Remove the bricks, one by one, over several weeks as the leaves reach the surface.

Choose plant containers for your specific needs.

Planting oxygenators

Most oxygenating plants are sold as bunches of unrooted cuttings with a weight at one end. To plant these, simply drop them in to the pond. Sometimes a stone attached to the bunch with an elastic band will help to carry them to the bottom. If you wish, you can loosely fill a container with soil. Insert about 7.5cm (3in) of the weighted end of the

Oxygenators should be added in weighted bunches.

cuttings into the soil, firm gently, add gravel and place into the pond.

Planting a bog garden

Bog garden plants are principally herbaceous perennial plants; their distinction from non-bog garden perennials is that they require a consistently moist soil. Plant them in spring or autumn (container plants are usually available from garden centres all year round). Mesh baskets are not necessary, so plant them directly into the soil. However, take care not to compact the wet soil when walking over it. Do not add fertilizers or handfuls of rotted or concentrated manures that may run in to the pond water. Plants growing in moist soil usually grow vigorously (think of the giant rhubarb, Gunnera, and ornamental rhubarb, Rheum), so give new plants plenty of space.

PLANT CARE

Keep pond plants healthy by following a programme of routine maintenance. Remember, however, that aquatic plants are generally more vigorous than other garden plants, so you will need to be more attentive. The most important job is the regular removal of dead and dying foliage, as this prevents the build-up of decaying matter and so a reduction in water quality.

Cutting back and thinning

Submerged plants can be thinned at any time of year when they become too crowded. Do this little and often to avoid excess disruption to the water and mud in the bottom, otherwise algae may result.

Floating plants, such as duckweed (Lemna) and fairy moss (Azolla), can be raked to the side and removed as necessary. Larger floating plants, such as water soldiers (Stratiotes), can have their younger plantlets removed and refloated as required.

Place a plant feeding tablet into the container.

Mulch around marginal plants with bark.

Overcrowded plants are more prone to pests and diseases, so regular division is important. Waterlilies need to be divided when their flowering starts to diminish. At this time their leaves become congested and are held vertically above the water. Dividing them is best done in summer, after flowering, every third or fourth year.

Deadheading

As with all other flowering garden plants, removing the faded blooms will lengthen the plants' flowering period. Some plants with single flushes of blooms may, after being deadheaded, produce a second flush. Deadheading also saves the plants' energy and in the case of certain potentially invasive plants, it will help to prevent their uncontrolled spread by self-seeding.

Dead flowerheads are usually removed with some of the flower stem attached, using secateurs or pond scissors. You could keep the faded flowerheads of some bog garden perennials – such as astilbes – over part of the winter, as these are quite attractive.

YEAR-ROUND PLANT MAINTENANCE GUIDE

Early winter

- Ponds should not be allowed to ice over, but if it does ice over, NEVER crack ice with a hammer as this can be deadly to fish. Melt a hole with a saucepan full of boiling water. Keep a section of the pond ice-free by running a fountain or waterfall permanently.

Mid-winter

- Tender pond plants (such as Eichhornia, the water hyacinth) that are lifted in autumn for storing indoors should be inspected regularly.
- Many people stop feeding fish in winter, while others believe that if the weather is mild and the fish are active, their reserves will be depleted if they do not eat. If the fish are swimming close to the surface, offer them a sprinkling of food; if they decline, then stop.

Late winter

- If you are thinking about making a new pond, or re-shaping or enlarging an existing one, this is a good time to do it.
- This is the time of year when frogs are mating – and there will be an abundance of frog spawn and tadpoles in your pond as a result. It is important to

ensure that any frogs, toads and newts can leave the pond when they need to.

Early spring

- Remove pond algae and decaying vegetation as and when you see it.
- Fish need careful nurturing to restore their normal strength and energy,

Thin or separate overgrown marginals in early spring.

and to improve their health generally in time for the breeding season. So start feeding them, but do not use too much food or it will contaminate the water.

Other jobs for early spring:

- If you take your submersible pump out of the pond for the winter, now is the time to re-install it
- Test the quality and pH of the water, and make any remedial treatments
- Feed containerized aquatic plants with appropriate pellets; feed established bog garden plants with general fertilizer, but do not allow it to enter the pond
- Lift and divide overgrown marginals
- Plant new plants in the bog garden

Mid-spring

- Give bog garden plants a little extra feed, but always use fertilizers with caution near a pond. Some plants may need staking at this time.

Other water garden jobs for mid-spring:
- Introduce new aquatic plants to your pond
- Divide overgrown waterlily clumps
- Try to rid your pond of algae and blanket weed
- Check for signs of slugs on bog garden plants and marginals, and treat as appropriate

Late spring

- Tidy the bog garden and remove dead or diseased foliage. Deadheading is important as it removes any places where mould can set in. By its nature a bog garden is damp and botrytis, grey mould and similar diseases may be more troublesome here than elsewhere.

Trim dead and dying material to keep plants healthy.

- If your pond fish have spawned, make sure that the fry have access to a shallow area.

Other water garden jobs for late spring:
- Check for signs of plant pests, and treat as appropriate

Early summer

- Water can be lost through evaporation, so keep the water level topped up regularly; the easiest way to do this is with a hose and a fine-spray attachment.
- In hot weather the fish can become lethargic, so reduce feeding slightly.

Other water garden jobs for early summer:
- Thin out overgrown clumps of oxygenators
- Weed the bog garden, and apply copious amounts of water during dry spells
- Check and cut back overgrown waterlilies

Mid-summer

- If you are away, ask a neighbour to switch on any aeration device for a short while during the period you are away. This will help to oxygenate the water. If you do not have a powered aeration device, running a hosepipe into the pond on muggy days will do some good.

Other water garden jobs for mid-summer:
- Pond levels may still need topping up
- Continue to remove blanket weed and other algae

Late summer

- Start a weekly routine of pulling out dead leaves and stems from your pond, before they sink to the bottom and give off harmful gases.

Your weekly tidying regime should be as follows:

- Cut and clear away any collapsing stems and leaves
- Trim back fading marginal plants by two-thirds
- Leave one or two areas as cover for various water animals that spend winter hiding near the banks
- Remove older leaves of waterlilies
- Watch for the two main waterlily pests: aphids and lily beetle. Fire a jet of water at the leaves to knock the pests off; remove the worst affected leaves

Other water garden jobs for late summer:

- Divide overgrown marginal plants
- Detach young portions of tender aquatic plants (such as Eichhornia) for overwintering safely indoors
- Tropical or tender fish should be returned to their winter quarters indoors

Early autumn

- Lift and divide any bog garden plants that need it – except the tenderest types, which are better left until spring. Leave waterlilies and other fully aquatic species until spring.
- Cut back clumps of marginal species. Leave long stumps, especially if they are a trifle tender and have hollow stems.
- Continue to feed fish regularly, but make sure they eat all that is given to them. Excess food will drop to the bottom and rot, so scatter a few flakes or pellets and supply more only if the first are completely devoured.

Mid-autumn

- If you prefer to remove the pump and store it over winter, then now is the time to disconnect it.
- Continue to collect leaves from the pond or water feature. Try not to disturb the mud too much.

A pond vacuum cleaner is a useful device to remove debris.

Other water garden jobs for mid-autumn:

- Continue to remove blanket weed and other algae
- As daylight lengths shorten, thin floating plants to allow as much sunlight on to the pond as possible

Late autumn

- This is a good time for building new ponds, free from the urgency of spring, the heat and dryness of summer and the cold and inhospitable ground conditions of winter.
- Water in the pond will reach 5°C (41°F), the critical point below which all feeding of fish should stop.

Other water garden jobs for late autumn:

- Check your liner (or concrete) for cracks and leaks
- Check for slippery paths and paving stones
- Prevent ice forming

PROPAGATION

DIVIDING PLANTS

Although you can divide plants in spring, autumn is arguably a better time, giving the plants a sufficient period before winter sets in.

Waterlilies

When waterlily leaves do not rest flat on the surface of the water, it is time to divide the plant. Take it out of its container and wash off the soil so that the rootstock is visible. Using a sharp knife, remove the side roots where they join the main stem, and dust the cut surface with a sulphur-based fungicide to help stop infection. Repot each piece of new, healthy root into its own container and cover the surface of the pot with pea shingle.

Remove marginals and cut away dead material.

Prise smaller plants apart by hand.

Floating plants

Dividing a floating water plant.

Floating plants can be lifted by hand or netted out. Some plants, such as water hyacinth (Eichhornia), produce young plantlets from the parent plants. During spring these can be snapped off. Place these offshoots directly onto the surface, supporting them with your hand until they find their floating levels.

Marginals

Marginal plants become overcrowded after three years or so, especially if they are grown in containers. Remove the plant from its basket. Cut away any dead or dying material. Smaller plants can be prised apart by hand,

Once divided, cut away any extraneous roots.

while others will need two garden forks to lever the plant apart and split the clump in two. Cut away any extraneous roots. Depending on the size of the original plant, this process can be repeated several times to result in smaller clumps.

TAKING CUTTINGS

Plants that can be propagated by division offer a fairly 'instant' result, whereas taking cuttings is a much longer process. The 'young plants' are unlikely to survive if they are placed straight into the pond.

Before they can be put into their final growing situations, cuttings will need looking after in a protected environment, perhaps under glass.

Soft stem cuttings

Some bog garden and marginal plants, including the marsh St John's wort (*Hypericum elodioides*) and brooklime (*Veronica beccabunga* – pictured below) can be propagated by soft stem cuttings.

Using a sharp knife, cut off from the parent plant a healthy, non-flowering shoot about 15cm (6in) long. Carefully strip off the lower leaves and any basal

sideshoots. Cut the stem squarely, just below a node (the spot where a leaf had grown). Dip the bottom into some rooting hormone powder or liquid and tap off any excess.

Remove the lower leaves of soft stem cuttings.

Fill a 10cm (4in) square fine mesh aquatic

container with aquatic compost. Insert the cutting and firm it in place. Water and cover the container with a clear plastic bag or place it in a propagator until you can see roots coming out of the bottom of the pot – not much more than two to three weeks.

Pot the cutting into a suitable growing medium.

Root bud cuttings

Tuberous and rhizomatous plants, such as waterlilies, flowering rush (*Butomus umbellatus*) and some irises, produce tiny new growing points on the rootstock. In mid- to late spring, sections of rootstock containing these buds can be removed from the parent plant, potted up and then grown on to produce a new plant.

Plant each section in its own 7.5cm (3in) or smaller pot, containing finely sifted soil or aquatic compost. Make sure the bud or growing tip is just visible. Then place the pot in a greenhouse or coldframe, in a tray with enough water in it to come over the rim of the pot. As the shoots grow, the young plants will need to be potted on and the water level raised accordingly.

Keep the plants in frost-free conditions over winter. By next spring they should be ready to plant out.

SOWING SEEDS

Most flowering aquatic and bog garden plants can be grown from seed. Plants are likely to take some time to grow to flowering size, so you'll need lots of patience.

Saving seed

A source of free seed is to collect from existing plants. Collect it when ripe, in summer or autumn usually. If it is not going to be sown immediately, it should be stored in small containers of water.

Sowing techniques

Fill a pot or seed tray with aquatic compost. Water it and then compress it with a small piece of flat wood. Thinly sow the seeds over the surface. Sieve a thin layer of fine horticultural sand over the surface. Stand the container in a large tray of water, and keep the

Do not overcrowd the seeds in the pot.

Sieve horticultural sand over the surface.

water topped up to the level of the compost.

Place the tray in a light position until the seeds have germinated. When the seedlings have a pair of true leaves beyond the seed-leaves, prick them out into their own small pots. Stand the trays in

Divide congested fern clumps in spring.

water, or keep the seedlings moist, as before. Pot on when a good root system has fully developed.

Ferns and Grasses

Divide congested clumps in spring for ferns and either spring or autumn for grasses.

Ferns can also be propagated by surface-sowing ripe spores – found on the underside of fronds –

Keep the water topped up to compost level.

under glass in autumn or spring. Collect the seed of species grasses when the flowerhead turns brown. Sow in autumn or spring, and if the former, make sure that seedlings are kept in a frost-free greenhouse over winter.

PLANTING COMBINATIONS

How should we plan a planting scheme in and around the pond, which looks good from the moment we conceive it until the full realization of it in the garden?

Understanding foliage

Although the success of any planting combination is ultimately a matter of personal preference, it is generally accepted that the best plant combinations are those in which, for example, large bold leaves

(such as hostas, rodgersias or lysichitons) are sited next to finer-foliaged plants (such as astilbes, primulas or even irises). Similarly, an attractive grass-like plant will sit very well next to a bold broad-leaved plant.

The colours of the leaves also plays an important role. For example, a plant with

Contrasts in colour and form matter in a water garden.

'normal' green leaves can be enhanced by its being placed next to a plant with variegated leaves. Similarly, the variegated plant will stand out when surrounded by plants which have plain coloured leaves.

Placing blue-leaved plants, such as *Hosta* 'Hadspen Blue' or *Festuca glauca* 'Elijah

Research which plants best suit your pond before buying them.

Blue' next to, or in the vicinity of, yellow-leaved plants such as *Hosta* 'Gold Edger' or *Carex elata* 'Aurea' can achieve a really pleasing combination.

Getting the timing right

Be aware, when planning a border or a planting scheme, of when certain plants do certain things. It is usually the aim of the gardener to grow as wide a variety of plants as possible, and to achieve colour and effect for as much of the year as possible.

Specifically, to grow a plant that flowers in early spring is perfectly acceptable, but to place it between two other plants that flower in early spring is perhaps a waste. Why not place this new subject somewhere else, possibly where colour is lacking at that time?

The flowering time of neighbouring plants is also critical if their colours are the same or similar. For example, a mid-summer flowering pink Astilbe next to a mid-summer flowering orange Hemerocallis would not be a good idea, as they both flower at the same time and the two colours clash. A mid-summer flowering pink Astilbe next to a late spring flowering orange Hemerocallis would be better, as the two plants will not be competing with each other.

Use of the water and surroundings

It is not a good idea to site tall trees and large shrubs near to a pond, because they cast shade over the water, which prohibits good aquatic plant and animal development.

But at the planning stage, planting near to or in the water can have its own sets of problems. Throughout this book we have examined which plants need to have their roots in water, and which merely prefer moist soil. It is critical to know this at the planning stage. It is also important to know which plants will grow upright and which will hang over the pond edge or even drape into the water.

Waterlilies, for example, have virtually no above-water height, and so you can plant them anywhere in the pond and they will not spoil other plants. However, after a couple of years a vigorous waterlily can swamp other, less aggressive, varieties. Waterlilies also do not like to be placed near fountains or waterfalls, as the constant water movement is debilitating to them.

One of the most attractive things about water is its ability to reflect. Reflection is a dimension unavailable in any other aspect of gardening, so we should exploit it. The reflection of plants growing in and around the pond can be enjoyed almost as much as the real above-water scene. A strategically placed garden ornament, bird-bath, sundial or similar structure can also be repeated in a watery reflection. But beware, so too can ugly nearby buildings or, if you are not careful, even the neighbour's washing line!

Use ornaments to enhance your planting scheme.

FISH, KOI & WILDLIFE

BUYING POND FISH

The urge to install fish in a new pond can be enormous. Resist it! Six weeks is not an unrealistic time to wait. During the first couple of weeks, fresh water in the pond will turn brown-green as micro-organisms multiply. A variety of plants should be put in place, including submerged oxygenators. These will help to absorb dissolved minerals and provide oxygen to the water. The fish will need these plants for both protection and as a source of green food. By the sixth week the water should be clear.

Take your time and choose the healthiest specimens.

Introducing fish to the pond

When you buy fish from a pet shop or aquatic centre, and then transport them home, they will be subjected to a considerable degree of stress. If the journey home is likely to take longer than four hours, the bag containing the fish should be opened in order for more oxygen to be made available to them. Fish are highly sensitive to changes in temperature and water quality, so avoid any shocks when transferring them to the pond. When you buy fish from a pet shop or aquatic centre they will be given to you in a plastic bag. For best results, follow this simple process:

1. Place the bag containing the fish in the pond, and leave it for 10 minutes so that the water temperature inside the bag reduces to the same as that of the pond water.
2. Introduce a little pond water into the bag. Leave it to stand for 10 minutes.
3. Add a little more water and leave for a further 10 minutes.
4. Push the bag on to its side so that the fish can swim away freely.

TIP: Before you buy pond fish you should know how many, and of what size, your pond can accommodate safely. This is a good guide: allow 155sq cm (24sq in) of water surface area per 2.5cm (1in) length of fish – excluding tails! Once the calculation has been made, reduce it by 25%, to allow for the fish to grow.

HARDY POND FISH SPECIES

The common goldfish is a fairly long-lived fish – a lifespan of 15 years is not unusual. Originally from China and parts of Siberia, the goldfish is able to withstand temperatures practically down to freezing. It can grow to 30cm (12in) from head to tail, if conditions are right, and the pool large enough.

These are some of the most commonly seen types of pond fish:

Shubunkins A graceful fish with large fins. The Bristol Shubunkin has a mottled coloration, often blueish.

Comet A sleeker cousin of the shubunkin, with a longer tail, often pointed.

Veiltail Oval-bodied, double-tailed with long fins.

Ranchu Oval-bodied, with a curved back profile minus the dorsal fin. Usually orange.

Moor Double-tailed black fish, sometimes with protruding eyes, rather more tender than the others. **Fantail** and **Oranda** are tender and at their best in a coldwater aquarium. However, they make good pond inhabitants for the warmer months.

The common goldfish is short-finned.

Golden orfe Perfect for larger ponds, these fish are fast movers, and enjoy the splashes from fountains.

Golden tench This fish can grow to 71cm (28in), although 30–41cm (12–16in) is more usual. Tench feed off the muddy bottoms of the pond.

Golden rudd Silver, with a golden hue, their scales are large and rough-looking. Fish can grow to 41cm (16in), feeding on worms, insects and aquatic vegetation.

Grass carp Most kept in ornamental pools are albinos. They can get large – over 1m (3ft) in length – so a large pond is required.

Feeding

Fish are generally omnivorous, naturally eating both plant and animal material.

Do not give your fish artificial feed (flakes or pellets) if the temperature drops below 5°C (41°F). It is harmful to

Your fish will live longer when fed specialist food.

feed fish when it is so cold as their metabolic processes, including digestion, slow right down, increasing the danger of food rotting inside the gut. When the water temperature stabilizes above 15°C (59°F), high protein feed can be used.

KEEPING KOI

Newcomers should spend time with fellow hobbyists or dealers: this is the best way to learn about the types of fish, the care they need, and the types of products needed to keep them healthy.

Identifying koi

Koi are referred to globally by their Japanese classes and variety names. The following is a simplified list of the various classes of metallic and non-metallic koi:

METALLIC

Hikarimono Single-coloured metallic koi often in gold, silver, yellow, orange, grey and platinum varieties.

Hikarimoyomono Metallic orange or yellow on white.

Hikariutsurimono Metallic forms of Utsuri and Showa. **Sanshoko koi** (see below).

NON-METALLIC

Kohaku Red markings on a white base. **Tancho Sanke** Red and black markings on a white base. **Showa Sanshoko** Red and white markings on a

A non-metallic Kohaku koi.

black base. **Bekko** Black markings on a red, yellow or white base colour. **Utsurimono** Red, yellow or white markings on a black base colour. **Asagi** and **Shusui** Body blue or dark blue, with red/orange belly. **Koromo** Red markings overlaid with darker pattering, on a white base colour. **Tancho** Single red spot

Tancho Sanke is one of the most popular breeds.

on the top of the head. **Kawarimono** All other forms of non-metallic koi, including single colours. **Kinginrin** Fish having shiny scales of any body type.

Avoiding koi 'stress'

Koi must live in a stress-free environment. There are many factors involved in fish stressing, such as:
Pollutants The water should be chemically clean.
Oxygen Most koi keepers incorporate an air pump.
Vitamins and minerals These must be supplemented by feeding good quality food, formulated for koi.
Heavy metals There should be low, or preferably zero, levels of the heavy metals such as lead, copper and zinc.
Temperature Keepers often add some form of heating to achieve stability of temperature.

ENCOURAGING WILDLIFE

In a balanced garden there should be a stable food chain of prey and predator. For example, a garden without any slugs is unlikely to have any frogs or toads (even if there is a pond). Low populations of most pests will help to encourage wildlife.

Amphibious wildlife

Frogs These are possibly our most welcome visitors, roaming the garden devouring slugs and other garden pests. Adults spend most of the summer living in moist, shaded vegetation, but never far from the water. From late winter, frogs begin spawning. Soon clumps of spawn are seen, turning into thousands of tadpoles within weeks. These feed on pond algae initially, but as they age they turn carnivore and eat small pond-dwelling invertebrates, including each other!

Frogs are a boon in the water garden.

Toads Mainly nocturnal feeders, common and natterjack toads are usually larger, wartier, rarer and more rounded in shape than frogs. Toads will eat slugs, caterpillars, beetles, woodlice and even ants. Mid- to late spring is when you will see strings of eggs, wound around the submerged pondweed.

Newts Smooth, crested and palmate newts are shy, secretive creatures, but they are just as beneficial as frogs and toads in terms of eating garden pests. Newts emerge from hibernation around mid-spring. Eggs are laid individually, usually in submerged foliage.

Leeches The most unpopular of all pond inhabitants, they suck the bodily fluids out of their prey. To avoid leeches in your pond, check any plants or fish you introduce. Most species feed on water snails and fish.

Insects

Damselflies and dragonflies The larvae of these beautiful creatures live under the water, feeding on small creatures passing by. They gradually climb out of the pond to emerge as adults. Damselflies are slightly daintier versions of the dragonfly, and it is possible to find red and blue versions of both.

Water boatman This familiar bug – actually a type of fly – swims just beneath the surface of the water. There are two main types: the lesser water boatman, which sieves organic matter from the water via hairs on its legs (it also uses its legs to rub together at

Pond skaters usefully cleanse the water surface.

mating time, rather like the grasshopper); and the greater water boatman, which is a predator, and can even bite!

Pond skaters These insects 'walk' on the surface of the water, spreading their weight over as large an area as possible. They feed on dead and dying insects, and effectively 'clean-up' the surface of the water for us, albeit on a minuscule scale.

Mosquitoes These pests prefer still waters to ponds with waterfalls and fountains; they lay eggs anywhere that is still. Fortunately the eggs and larvae are considered delicious by fish; you will therefore often find greater populations of mosquitoes wherever there is an absence of fish.

Mammals, birds and others

A host of mammals will also visit your pond. Many of these creatures will arrive at night, so you will not always see them. Their presence, however, forms part of the rich diversity that makes keeping a wildlife pond so enjoyable.

Animals – from hedgehogs (which are actually good swimmers), through to foxes, badgers and even fully grown deer – will visit your pond, provided they live in your vicinity and have access to the water.

All types of garden birds will seek out shallow areas where they can splash about in sunny weather – even during winter, for the cold does not deter them from taking a bath. Less welcome birds, such as herons, will also make regular calls, as long as there is a ready supply of food available to them.

Freshwater snails will probably need to be introduced to your pond (they can be purchased from aquatic centres or they may come in unwittingly with water plants). They usually feed on decaying plant matter and algae. There are many different species of snail, some of which are tiny.

TIPS:

- **Do** create an area of rockery near to the pond.
- **Don't** have pools with steep sides, which makes it difficult for animals to get out of the water.
- **Do** create a central island within the pond.
- **Don't** put the pond near to large trees.
- **Do** allow dead wood to become a feature of your pond.
- **Do** – and perhaps this is the most important 'do' of all – create a sitting area, where you can observe (and feed) the wildlife at close quarters.

WATER GARDEN PROBLEMS

All ponds and water features will at some time suffer problems. Rectifying these problems is entirely possible but might take time.

ACID WATER

When fish are prone to sudden death and red fins, this is a sure sign that the water has a high level of acidity (or low pH). Remedy: see 'Alkaline water' below.

ALKALINE WATER

When fish are prone to fungal diseases and gill disorders, this is a sure sign that the water has a high level of alkalinity (or high pH). Remedy: Whether the water is biased towards acidity or alkalinity, the remedial process is the same. To correct the pH level to the desired level of pH7–7.5, change about 25% of the water in the pond. Then increase the aeration level.

GREEN WATER

Caused by a vast number of microscopic algae, this is not harmful to fish or plants but is unsightly. In new ponds this effect should clear by itself. If not install a filter with UV clarifier, and then when the water has cleared by half or more add more oxygenating plants to get a desirable 'balance' of plants and fish.

SMELLY WATER

A balanced pond with fish, plants, and perhaps a fountain will have enough 'going on' to prevent the build up of gases. If your pond has just a faint odour, then reduce the water level by about half, and use a pond vacuum to suck up the silt and detritus from the bottom of the pond. Then, top up with clean water. If the problem is acute, drain the pond (after first netting out any fish), extract the silt, and refill it with clean water. Installing a filter with UV clarifier should help to prevent this from happening again.

LEAKING CONCRETE POND

To trace the leak turn off all pumps and filters, and allow the water to drop to the level from where it is escaping. The leak may be in the rendering or it may be in the base concrete, due to plant roots growing through it. Repair a small leak with rendering. Where the leak is more serious it may be necessary to install a butyl liner, which will maintain the water in the pond.

POND ICING OVER

The ice layer prevents oxygen from getting in to the water. Melt a hole with a saucepan full of boiling water. Prevent ice from forming in the first place by using an electric pool heater, or run a fountain or waterfall permanently – the moving water never becomes still enough for ice to form.

PESTS & DISEASES

Like other garden plants, aquatics and bog garden types are subject to the ravages of specific pests and diseases.

BLACKFLY/GREENFLY
In a water garden situation these should be referred to more correctly as waterlily aphids. If plants are infested, spray the leaves forcefully with a jet of water to wash the flies into the pond where fish will eat them.

WATERLILY BEETLE
The small brown beetles are the most damaging pest of waterlilies. The adult beetle lays its eggs on the leaves, then the blackish larvae emerge. These grubs eat the leaves, making holes on the edges and centre. Cut away badly affected leaves, and hose the grubs into the water.

CADDIS FLY
The larva of this insect chews into the roots of aquatic plants to make a shelter. It only becomes serious if a large number of the grubs are present. There is no recommended treatment for the control of the flies.

IRIS SAWFLY
The larva of this insect is a bluish maggot, which feeds on the leaves of irises. Remove seriously damaged

leaves, and pick off and destroy any grubs seen. Where bog garden irises are affected, an application of derris dust will help to control the pest.

LEAFHOPPERS
These small, green, hopping insects move from plant to plant, and they do most damage to soft, fleshy-leaved marginals at the edges of our ponds. Affected leaves will have small pale yellow-green spots on the upper leaf surfaces. Hose the grubs into the water.

SLUGS/GARDEN SNAILS
These do not cause a problem in the water, but they can devour precious plants at the water's edge or in the bog garden. Chemical control can be harmful to birds and other creatures that might be tempted to eat the deceased molluscs. Laying beer or orange peel traps overnight is a more environmentally friendly, if unpleasant form of control. Bog gardens are unfortunately perfect breeding grounds for these pests.

VINE WEEVILS
Bog garden plants are at risk here; the adult weevils gnaw holes in leaves of hostas, aruncus, astilbes and sometimes primulas. The cream coloured grubs are more damaging in that they eat the roots of certain plants, often causing the death of the plant. Remove and destroy the adult weevils by hand.

A–Z DIRECTORY

This A–Z directory incorporates a selection of plants from the various categories of aquatic plants that could be chosen for different water gardens (by this we mean ponds, water containers, lakes, bog gardens and wildlife pond gardens). Broadly speaking, the various groups are: oxygenating plants, floating aquatics, flowering aquatics, marginal plants and bog garden plants. The following plants should give both the novice and experienced water gardener a good enough selection to grace any water garden.

Water can be combined with floral colour for stunning effects.

ACORUS

Sweet flag

The leaves of this popular hardy herbaceous plant were often used to cover the floors of castles before the introduction of carpets; the 'sweet' part of the name refers to the pleasing aroma – reminiscent of cinnamon or citrus – which comes from the leaves when they are crushed. The plant's rhizome also contains oil that is extracted for use in the perfume industry.

Acorus calamus 'Argenteostriatus'

Although small, green-brown insignificant flowers are carried at the tops of the stems on mature plants during early to mid-summer, it is the foliage that is the main feature. The all-green leaves of the straight species give it the appearance of an iris, but it is in no way related. Deciduous, arching, iris-like leaves up to 2.5cm (1in) wide have a very pronounced mid-rib. In warm climates, reddish seeds are formed in mid-summer.

Its less vigorous variegated form is the one most often seen. *Acorus calamus* 'Argenteostriatus' (formerly 'Variegatus') starts with pink and cream shoots in early spring, which turn into gold and cream striped leaves.

A. gramineus (referred to as the Dwarf Japanese Rush, although the plant is not technically a rush) is approximately a third of the size of *A. calamus*, and has vertical green and white striped grass-like leaves. It remains evergreen in all but the harshest of conditions.

Forms of *A. calamus* can grow rather large, so are best suited to larger ponds. If kept in smaller ponds the plants will require regular trimming back.

In spring, plant rhizomes directly into the soil, preferably in water 8–25cm (3–10in) deep. Choose a site that is in full sun or very light shade.

KEY FACTS

Flowers small, green-brown and insignificant; early to mid-summer **Plant** early–late spring **Site** in a pond situated in full sun or light shade **Min Temp** -20°C **Height** 40–120cm **Spread** 35–75cm

CARE: To propagate, which is very easy, simply cut off a piece of healthy rhizome in spring and plant it immediately in mud at the recommended depth.

AJUGA REPTANS

Bugle

Ajuga is a shade-loving plant that is excellent for growing under trees and shrubs – as long as the soil stays quite moist. The irony is that the leaves are not seen at their best when the plant is growing in a shady place. Yet if you transfer the plant to a sunnier spot, it sulks and never performs. During winter, the leaf rosettes close up and the larger outer leaves drop away, leaving the creeping stems (stolons) with plantlets at their tips, cleary visible. Bugle is particularly suitable for growing between the paving of an informal pond surround.

KEY FACTS

Flowers purple to blue; early to mid-summer
Plant early–late spring and mid- to late autumn
Site bog gardens
Min Temp -20°C
Height 15cm
Spread 90cm

CARE: Give a little general fertilizer in spring and water well in dry periods. Propagate by division in spring. Plant individual plantlets directly into soil.

Ajuga reptans
'Burgundy Glow'

ALCHEMILLA

Lady's mantle

This is one of the most familiar of border plants, and is beloved of flower arrangers for the soft, wispy green flowers and thick uniquely serrated leaves. For the gardener it is a fine, architectural hardy herbaceous perennial. Its suitablility for the bog garden is a matter of conjecture; for some gardeners it seems to thrive in the moist confines of a bog, whereas for others it fades rapidly, seeming to prefer a sunny, dry spot. Make sure it is an open soil with plenty of humus; a waterlogged, anaerobic soil is almost certainly a deadly combination for Alchemilla.

KEY FACTS
Flowers yellow-green; early to late summer
Plant early–late spring
Site bog garden, in moist, open soil
Min Temp -20°C
Height 15–50cm
Spread 30–60cm

Alchemilla mollis

CARE: Mulch around the base of the plant in spring/autumn. Add general fertilizer in spring. Remove faded flowerheads and cut old growth back to ground level the end of autumn.

APONOGETON DISTACHYOS
Water hawthorn or *Cape weed*

This is an excellent plant for deep-water ponds. It has attractive floating leaves that are more or less evergreen; and the vanilla-like fragrance of the blooms is powerful and lingering. The leaves are oval, long, and mid-green with brown blotches, floating on the

Aponogeton distachyos

surface of the water. You do not need a full-sized pond in order to grow Aponogeton: even a water barrel could sustain a plant or two. They perform well in full sun, but with light shade they have a longer flowering period. Remove dead foliage as it appears.

CARE: Set out in spring, by planting tubers/young plants 45cm (18in) apart, in small groups in baskets, or directly into soil. Sow seeds in autumn straight away.

KEY FACTS

Flowers white; spring and mid-autumn
Plant early autumn/late spring
Site full sun/light shade
Min Temp -5°C
Height 10cm
Spread 60cm

ARUM

Woodland arum

Arum makes an ideal plant for any bog garden. The longest period of attraction is the foliage, with its pretty marbling. Next are its flowers – greenish spathes, each with a creamy white interior. This plant finally provides autumn colour with its stout spikes carrying clusters of the brightest deep-orange berries. A moist, but not waterlogged soil, is preferred. Plant the tubers roughly 15cm (6in) deep or, for young plants, up to the soil mark on the stem base. To propagate, divide the plants in spring or autumn. Collect and sow seed: save the fresh, ripe fruits and sow in a soil-based compost under glass.

Arum italicum

KEY FACTS
Flowers greenish cream; mid–late spring
Plant spring and mid–late autumn
Site bog gardens
Min Temp -15°C
Height 35–55cm
Spread 30–45cm

CARE: Little care is required once established, but it is useful if a handful of general fertilizer is applied around the base of the plant in spring.

ARUNCUS DIOICUS   *Goat's beard*

The feathery flowerheads of goat's beard are most unexpected for something that is in the same plant family as the rose. The elegant leaves, majestic flowers and tall stems make this plant an erect and stately star of the bog garden. The normal species needs plenty of room in which to spread. In early and mid-summer, tiny, cream-white blooms appear on large fluffy flowerheads. Arguably, Aruncus is just as attractive in the early flower stage, when the stems are delicately lined with tiny round buds, as it is when the great creamy plumes have exploded into foaming flowers.

Aruncus dioicus

CARE: Cut back the dead top growth in late autumn. Mulch soil-grown plants with compost in the spring or autumn. Add general fertilizer in the spring.

KEY FACTS

Flowers tiny, cream-white; early–mid-summer
Plant early–late spring
Site bog garden, light shade
Min Temp -20˚C
Height 100–200cm
Spread 60–120cm

ASTILBE

These plants seem to appear in almost every garden – whether or not it has a bog area. They are even planted in places that are distinctly unsuited to them. However, astilbes are the most accommodating of plants. They are colourful, easy, dramatic and stately, as well as being tough and hardy.

From mid-spring onwards the deeply cut leaves appear, often with purplish or bronzy green tints. Flowering generally begins in early summer. Attractive plume-like heads of tiny flowers are followed by the rusty-brown seedheads in late summer and autumn.

Between them, the species and hybrids provide numerous forms, from dwarf to tall, and in a multitude of shades. The hybrids borne out of *Astilbe* x *arendsii* are the most commonly seen, and these generally produce plumes up to 1m (3ft) in height. One of the best is the bright pink 'Bressingham Beauty'. For possibly the purest white *arendsii* hybrid, choose 'White Queen'. The

species *A. simplicifolia* has added its quota to the range of hybrids. The species is pretty, with graceful pink spikes 37cm (15in) tall, but 'Atrorosea' is

Astilbe x *arendsii* 'Venus'

superb, carrying sheaves of tiny bright pink flowers for a long time.

There are a couple of varieties from *A. japonica* that are worth mentioning. The white 'Deutschland' is regularly

Astilbe 'Deutschland'

used for forcing as pot plants and 'Etna' carries beautiful rich red plumes above mounded foliage.

Where height variations are important there should be room for beauties such as *A. chinensis tacquetii* 'Superba'. This grows to 1.5m (5ft), with spikes of bright rosy purple and a long season in flower.

A. chinensis pumila has a creeping habit of crispy leaves, close to the ground, and stumpy 30cm (12in) spikes of lilac rose, and is less fussy about its moisture needs than most.

KEY FACTS

Flowers white, pink, mauve, red; summer

Plant spring/mid-autumn

Site moist soil, light to moderate shade

Min Temp -20°C

Height 20–150cm

Spread 30–75cm

CARE: Moisture around the roots is very important. Mulch with well-rotted compost when the plants are dormant. Shelter from strong winds helps prolong the flowering period.

AZOLLA FILICULOIDES   *Fairy moss*

This is neither a moss, nor a flowering plant, but a tiny fern that collects into dense masses. Pale blue-green, lacy deciduous fronds, 1cm (½in) across, turn rich reddish purple during autumn. The short and slender roots absorb nourishment from the pond water. Site Azolla in full sun or light shade. In spring, drop a few fronds directly onto the water, but not in moving water. Plants survive winter as submerged dormant buds, but as frost injury is possible overwinter plantlets under glass in water and soil. Propagate by removing a few fronds in mid-spring and introduce them to a new pond.

Azolla filiculoides

KEY FACTS
Foliage pale blue-green turning purple during autumn
Plant early spring
Site full sun/partial shade
Min Temp -5˚C
Height 2.5cm
Spread 100+cm

CARE: It is a prolific spreader, so do not introduce into large, inaccessible ponds as it will rapidly become out of hand. Net out unwanted plants during the growing season.

BUTOMUS UMBELLATUS *Flowering rush or Water gladiolus*

Perfectly at home in the shallow waters of a still pool, the leaves are narrow, grass-like and purplish when young, gradually turning green. The white-flowered *Butomus umbellatus* 'Schneeweibschen' is excellent. Then there is the deeper pink *B. umbellatus* 'Rosenrot', which is stunningly beautiful. However, this variety may be more difficult to find. During spring, plant in a basket with a high level of clay or at least a heavy loam soil. Set in a water depth of 2.5–15cm (1–6in). Cut down all growth in autumn.

Butomus umbellatus

KEY FACTS
Flowers small, rose-pink blooms; mid- to late summer
Plant early–late spring
Site full sun/light shade
Min Temp -20˚C
Height 90cm
Spread 60cm

CARE: Divide overgrown clumps every couple of years in spring or sow seeds under glass in autumn – germination rates, however, are usually poor, so you may not be lucky.

CALLA PALUSTRIS

Bog arum

This extremely hardy perennial is at home either as a marginal plant or as a shallow water aquatic. It is ideal for concealing the sides of a man-made pond – its stout rhizomes colonizing the shallows and supporting a lush dense carpet of leaves. Arguably, the autumn berries – which are poisonous – are even more attractive looking than the flowers.

The flowers are tiny and yellow-green, studded on a cylindrical spike enclosed by a prominent bright white funnel-shaped, arum-like spathe. Water snails are thought to be instrumental in pollinating the flowers. Broadly heart-shaped, glossy thick rich-green leaves are carried on long stalks growing from strong creeping rhizomes. Normally only this single species is available.

Planting should take place during spring, placing pieces of the rhizomes 23cm (9in) apart directly into wet soil or in baskets. Choose a position in full sun or light shade, in wet soil at the edge of larger ponds, or in shallow water to a depth of 20cm (8in).

If planted in baskets, these plants will not spread so rapidly and are easier to keep in check.

CARE: Divide rhizomes in spring, either transplant directly into the pond or start them into growth in trays of mud under glass before planting out.

Calla palustris

Cut down dead foliage in autumn and winter. Keep the plants healthy by dividing the larger clumps every four or five years.

The arum lily (*Zantedeschia aethiopica*) is formerly *Calla aethiopica* and is often referred to as the calla lily; it is a close relation, and an extremely valuable marginal and bog garden plant in its own right (see page 187).

Calla palustris originates throughout Northern Europe, Siberia and North America; in Lapland, the rhizomes of the bog arum are dried, ground and processed to be used as a kind of flour for baking in Finnish 'missebroed'.

KEY FACTS
Flowers yellow-green on white spathe; late spring to early summer
Plant early–late spring
Site full sun/light shade
Min Temp -20°C
Height 30cm
Spread 60cm

CALTHA PALUSTRIS   *Marsh marigold or Golden kingcup*

This aquatic 'buttercup' is one of the most familiar plants for pondside planting. With deep golden flowers and large, rounded leaves, its appeal derives from its neat habit: Caltha does not become straggly and unkempt in the way so many marginals do.

From mid-spring to early summer, golden yellow, waxy buttercup-like blooms appear, proud of the glossy, dark green deciduous leaves. These leaves are more or less rounded, and carried on long stalks.

During early spring, Caltha should be planted directly into the soil at the edge of the pond. It prefers a position in full sun, but grows very well in medium shade; it is often found naturally in waterlogged woodland soils.

If you have a small pond you can only really grow single plants. If planting directly into soil under water, there should be a maximum water depth of 15cm (6in). For a more

Caltha palustris

impressive display, plant three or more plants together, about 30cm (12in) apart (obviously the size of the pond will dictate whether this is possible).

To propagate, sow fresh seed in late summer or early autumn in wet soil. Alternatively, divide the spreading roots of larger clumps in summer, after the flowers have faded.

Although most gardeners grow the single-flowered species, there are also the tightly double-flowered *Caltha palustris* 'Flore Pleno', which is free-flowering, and the single-flowered white form, *C. palustris* var. *alba*. This latter plant is slightly more compact and therefore ideal for smaller ponds. *C. leptosepala* is also better placed for small ponds; it has rather dainty star-like, golden-centred white flowers. A larger and more vigorous form of *C. palustris* is available, and as if to emphasize its stature, it is called *C. palustris* var. *palustris*.

KEY FACTS

Flowers golden yellow, white; mid-spring to early summer
Plant early–late spring
Site full sun/light shade
Min Temp -20˚C
Height 60–75cm
Spread 50–60cm

CARE: There is little maintenance required with this plant, only to remove dead foliage when seen and give a general tidy-up in the autumn.

CAREX

Carex elata 'Aurea' is one of the few sedges that is non-invasive enough to grow in an average-sized bog garden. The brownish flowers are quite uninspiring, but the evergreen leaves are the main reason for growing the plant. By the end of spring, after flowering, the plant throws up long, arching leaves of the strongest yellow colour of all grass-like plants, whether grown in dry soil or a bog garden. A narrow green margin to each blade makes the plant quite spectacular. The colour deepens until late summer, when it fades gradually to green.

Carex elata 'Aurea'

KEY FACTS
Flowers brownish; mid- to late spring
Plant early–mid-spring/mid-autumn
Site full sun/light shade
Min Temp -20˚C
Height 45–50cm
Spread 45cm

CARE: Mulch in autumn and spring; give a general fertilizer in spring. Leave top growth over winter, and cut it down in early spring. Divide clumps every five or six years.

COTULA

Brass buttons or
Golden buttons

Cotula is grown either as a short-lived tender perennial, but more often as an annual. The fine, shiny, light green leaves, which are also aromatic, make the plant ideally suited to hiding the edges of ponds and bare soil in containers. Plant young plants or transplant self-sown seedlings in late spring. A position in full sun is best, in water 0–10cm (0–4in) deep. To propagate, simply allow it to self-seed and transplant the seedlings to better places as soon as they are large enough to move.

Cotula coronopifolia

KEY FACTS
Flowers golden yellow; late spring to early autumn
Plant early–late spring
Site full sun
Min Temp -10°C
Height 15–20cm
Spread 30–45cm

CARE: Control self-seeding by removing old flowers, before seeds have time to form. Remove excess or frost-damaged foliage to prevent it from falling in and polluting the water.

EICHHORNIA CRASSIPES

Water hyacinth

This is a robust, free-floating plant and a prolific spreader in hot climates. Bluish-violet blooms, like small hyacinths, rise above the water surface from mid-summer to early autumn. Remove water hyacinths from the pond during mid-autumn. Divide and store them in wet mud or moist pots in a greenhouse or coldframe until the spring. They can be re-sited in the pond from mid-spring onwards, but it is worth hardening them off gradually; the plant tissue will have become tender, and could be damaged if there is a severe late frost.

Eichhornia crassipes

CARE: To propagate water hyacinths, separate the clumps in spring, or in the autumn as they are removed to their winter quarters, for best results.

KEY FACTS

Flowers blue-violet; mid-summer to early autumn
Plant late spring–early summer
Site full sun/light shade
Min Temp 5°C
Height 30cm
Spread 100cm

ELEOCHARIS

Hairgrass

Hairgrass plants (forms of Eleocharis) are usually regarded as submerged plants for aquaria rather than outdoor ponds; the hardier forms can also be grown as bog garden plants. A good outdoor oxygenator is *Eleocharis acicularis*. It spreads over the soil at the bottom of the pond or the soil in a planting basket with

Eleocharis acicularis

dense tufts of grass-like leaves, giving the impression of an underwater lawn. In reality, the delicate beauty of the leaves tends to be lost among the other, more vigorous and broader-leaved oxygenators.

CARE: Propagation is easy – during the growing season, break away clumps and replant. Divide into small plants before planting 2–5cm apart.

KEY FACTS
Flowers tiny greeny-brown; summer
Plant early–late spring
Site bog garden/pond in good light
Min Temp -10°C
Height 10–15cm
Spread 5–30cm

ELODEA

Canadian pond weed

Elodea canadensis is probably the most commonly seen oxygenator; it is hardy, vigorous and ideal for new ponds. Lance-shaped dark green leaves are held on long stems. It is one of the most efficient of all oxygenating plants, but it can also be invasive. However, it is worth trying if you have a small pond where other oxygenators have failed to establish. If it is confined to a planting basket, it can be easily controlled. Use in contained water features, such as a tub, barrel or glazed pot. It is a favourite food of goldfish and koi.

Elodea canadensis

KEY FACTS
Flowers greeny-white; early to late summer
Plant early–late spring
Site direct sunlight for at least part of the day
Min Temp -10°C
Height 10cm
Spread 50+cm

CARE: Elodea prefers water that is alkaline and grows best when planted in soil containing a high proportion of fine sand. Trim regularly to maintain its spread.

ERIOPHORUM

Cotton grass

Suited both to the bog garden and the margins of a pond, it is extremely slow growing, and is quite unmistakeable in summer when its seedheads form cottonwool-like tufts.

CARE: Keep the plants healthy by dividing the larger clumps every four or five years. To propagate, transplant the divisions directly or in trays of mud.

Choose a position in wet peaty acid soil at the edge of larger ponds or in shallow water no deeper than 10cm (4in). Plant 23cm (9in) apart directly into wet soil or into baskets. It is an undemanding plant, as long as it has acid soil and water. If growing in the bog garden as opposed to growing in water, mulch in spring and feed with a general fertilizer. If space permits, cotton grass should be planted in bold drifts at the edge of a wildlife pond to create a natural effect.

KEY FACTS

Flowers bright yellow, early to mid-spring; seedpods in summer
Plant early–late spring
Site full sun/light shade
Min Temp -20˚C
Height 60–75cm
Spread 100+cm

Eriophorum angustifolium

EUPATORIUM

Hemp agrimony

This is an excellent plant for attracting bees and butterflies to the bog garden, with its mass of feather-like flowers. Eupatorium is not a grand or stately plant, but it does show itself off well in an informal situation, and because of its propensity for attracting wildlife, it is worth making room for. Coarse, oval leaves are arranged along the full length of the tall stems. To propagate, sow seed in the autumn.

Eupatorium cannabinum 'Chocolate'

KEY FACTS

Flowers cream-white, rose-purple; mid-summer to mid-autumn
Plant early spring
Site bog garden, full sun
Min Temp -20˚C
Height 150–200cm
Spread 60cm

CARE: Mulch in spring and autumn. In late autumn, after the foliage has started to die back, cut any remaining growth right down to soil level.

FESTUCA GLAUCA

Little fescue

Although often thought of as plants for the dry border, in a sunny place, on a moist but never waterlogged soil, these grasses will do very well. The Festuca genus contains some 50 or so species and cultivars. The most popular of the little blue fescues is *Festuca glauca* 'Elijah Blue'. *F. glauca* 'Golden Toupee' forms tight cushions of soft, needle-like leaves that are almost iridescent yellow in spring, later fading to a yellowish green. As with the blue form, the flowers are the same colour as the leaves, but turning beige or brown as they fade.

Festuca glauca 'Elijah Blue'

KEY FACTS

Flowers yellow, silvery-blue, green; late spring to early summer
Plant early–late spring
Site moist soil in full sun
Min Temp -20°C
Height 10–35cm
Spread 15–60cm

CARE: All forms of *F. glauca* are useful for edging or as foreground groups – massed or spaced. Best foliage colour is maintained by dividing the clumps every two or three years.

FILIPENDULA

Meadowsweet

The most frequently seen form of meadowsweet is the European *Filipendula ulmaria*, which is ideal for all but the smallest of bog gardens. It is a tall, moisture-loving, bushy plant that works well around the edge of a pond. For the smaller garden choose *F. ulmaria* 'Aurea', a white-flowered cultivar that only grows 30cm (12in) high. 'Flore Pleno' produces unusual white flowers that are double. *F. rubra* 'Venusta' needs plenty of room, but is a superb plant in the right place. Dark green leaves are overtopped by large feathery deep rose pink flowers on tall stems.

Filipendula rubra 'Venusta'

KEY FACTS

Flowers white, rose; mid- to late summer
Plant early–late spring
Site light, shady bog garden
Min Temp -20°C
Height 30–200cm
Spread 20–90cm

CARE: Mulch in spring and autumn, and apply a general fertilizer to the root area in spring. Cut down dead foliage and stems in autumn.

GENTIANA

Gentian

Gentiana pneumonanthe is a moisture-loving member of this genus which produces clusters of rich, deep blue trumpet-shaped flowers. They appear at the ends of the stems during mid- to late summer. No other bog garden plant will provide as intense a blue as this unusual but very choice wild flower.

G. pneumonanthe (also known as Marsh gentian) is a dramatic blue gentian found wild right across the Northern Hemisphere. The flowers are large and trumpet-shaped, sometimes also resembling bells or urns. The leaves are lush green, shiny and lance-shaped on short, slender stems. For this plant to thrive and achieve its full impact, the soil needs to be kept damp and rich in organic matter and, perhaps most important of all, needs to have an acid pH.

Gentiana pneumonanthe

A position in full sun or light to moderate shade is required. The best time to plant is during spring. Straight after planting, mulch with garden compost, and do this annually each spring, along with a feed of general fertilizer. This gentian resents disturbance, so leave it well alone once it is established. Like other late-flowering gentians, *G. pneumonanthe* associates well with small, late-flowering bulbs, as well as ferns and grasses.

The willow gentian (*G. asclepiadea*) produces typical gentian-blue flowers on stems up to 60cm (24in) high, and tolerates some lime in the soil; it also has a white form, *G. asclepiadea* var. *alba*, and various pink or pale blue varieties.

To increase stock of both forms of gentian, take softwood cuttings in summer, rooting them in a propagator with slight bottom heat. Seeds can be sown in early spring, again in a propagator, and kept at around 20°C (68°F).

KEY FACTS

Flowers deep/pale blue, pink, white; mid- to late summer

Plant early–late spring

Site full sun/light shade

Min Temp -20°C

Height 30–90cm

Spread 25–60cm

CARE: If the leaves turn yellow in summer, the soil is not acid enough, so water it with sequestered iron to restore the pH levels.

GEUM RIVALE

Water avens

This is a hardy woodland plant, which enjoys a wetter soil than most of the garden geums. There are several selected forms and hybrids of *Geum rivale*, but these can be difficult to find. Plant out in spring or autumn in a lightly shaded spot. If planting more than one, set them out 30cm (12in) apart. These plants are more or less self-sufficient. They do not require staking. Cut down old foliage in late autumn. To propagate, divide the plants in autumn or spring; after three or four years they will need to be split anyway.

Geum rivale

KEY FACTS
Flowers pinkish-purple; late spring to early summer
Plant spring/mid-autumn
Site full sun/light shade
Min Temp -20°C
Height 15–45cm
Spread 20cm

CARE: Mulch around the root areas in autumn using moist, well-rotted garden compost. A little extra food, in the form of bone meal, should be applied in early spring.

GLYCERIA MAXIMA   *Striped manna grass*

This is the perfect waterside grass if you have lots of room in your garden. Despite its somewhat rampant nature, this is one of the most beautifully variegated of all grasses, both when viewed from close up and from a distance. The soft, blunt-tipped leaves, which can be as much as 60cm (2ft) long and some 5cm (2in) across, are cream, narrowly green-striped and tinged with a pink flush in spring. In autumn, just before the leaves fade away, they take on purple tints.

Glyceria maxima
var. *variegata*

KEY FACTS

Flowers creamy-white; mid-summer to early autumn

Plant early–late spring

Site full sun/light shade

Min Temp -20˚C

Height 90cm

Spread 100+cm

CARE: Apply a mulch for the plants in autumn and spring until they are established. Lift and divide overgrown plants at any time, as they can spread indefinitely.

GUNNERA

Giant rhubarb

The most familiar gunnera is *Gunnera manicata*. It is the largest of any hardy herbaceous plant; many call it the giant or prickly rhubarb, because of the similarity of its leaves. As long as there is sufficient space, even in a small garden, gunnera will help to create an exotic atmosphere. Gunneras are tolerant of most soils, but prefer deep, fertile soils with high moisture content. Feed with a general fertilizer in spring. They are undemanding plants, as long as they have some shelter from the coldest of winds and the latest of frosts.

Gunnera manicata

KEY FACTS

Flowers greenish-brown; late spring to early summer
Plant early–late spring
Site full sun/light shade
Min Temp -10˚C
Height 10–300cm
Spread 100–500cm

CARE: Cut back the dry leaves in autumn. In colder areas, protect the plants with straw or sacking; you can even use the old leaves to cover the plants.

HAKONECHLOA

Hakone grass

This is the perfect plant for the smaller garden, as it is slow-growing, compact and non-invasive. It can be a most striking plant when the sun shines on its brightly coloured leaves. Its size and grace make it attractively informal, yet its arching leaves and hemispherical shape conspire to give it almost perfect symmetry, making it ideal for the formal garden as well. Give shelter from cold, drying winds and apply a general fertilizer in spring. Every three or four years, lift and divide plants.

Hakonechloa macra
'Aureola'

KEY FACTS
Flowers reddish-brown; early autumn to early winter
Plant early–late spring
Site light shade
Min Temp -20°C
Height 20–40cm
Spread 30–60cm

CARE: Mulch around the plants in autumn and spring. Plant directly into the soil in the bog garden. If planting more than one, do not place them closer together than 25cm (10in).

HEMEROCALLIS

Daylily

Daylilies are so called because each individual flower lasts only a day. Plants can be grown in any part of the garden, but they perform best in reasonably moist soil, making luxuriant additions to any bog garden. The appeal of these plants is added to by the fact that they are so easy to grow and propagate.

The individual trumpet-shaped flowers are not particularly attractive in their own right, especially when they are a day old and are on the wane. The real beauty is when you see a mass of flowers. The varieties that produce flowers of a single colour are more attractive than those that have their main colour concentrated inside the trumpet, where it can only be seen if the flower is looked at end on. Also, nearly all the yellow varieties are scented, whereas most of the others are lacking this attribute.

The single coloured flowers, where the colour is repeated on the outside of the trumpet, give a much more effective impression and

Hemerocallis '**Pink Charm**'

Hemerocallis 'Black Magic'

make a more impressive statement in a border. But beware of some of the 'red' varieties (there is no true scarlet or carmine yet available): they can look very scrappy en masse and add nothing positive to the overall effect of the border.

The rushy leaves are a feature in their own right in spring: the brightest of greens, arching and growing almost 3cm (1in) a day. At flowering time the leaves are fully complementary to the trumpet flowers, which are produced on smooth stems.

Although there are several species available, these tend to be found only in specialists' gardens or nurseries. The earliest to show colour, in late spring, is the dwarf species *Hemerocallis dumortierii*, which has yellow flowers lasting for several weeks. *H. citrina* and *H. lilioasphodelus* are charming, fragrant yellow species for late spring and early summer. Another species of note, *H. multiflora*, produces

CARE: Cut away all foliage, right back to soil level, in the autumn. If you leave this the foliage will simply turn to an untidy mess over winter.

pale orange-yellow flowers in great profusion from mid-summer to mid-autumn.

Here is a list of some of the best garden hybrids. H.'Orangeman', first bred in 1906, has deep orange coloured flowers. H.'Hyperion' was introduced over 50 years ago, and is still in demand for its clear colour and large yellow flowers; a newer and outstanding yellow colour is the hybrid H.'Lark Song'. Then there is H.'Black Magic', with its deep ruby mahogany flowers; H.'Contessa', which produces light orange blooms; H.'Bonanza', with its soft yellow colour but a dwarf hybrid, matching well with the deeper coloured H.'Golden Chimes', which is also dwarf.

H.'Dubloon' (also sold as 'Golden Orchid') produces rich golden coloured flowers. The old variety H.'Pink Damask' still holds its own as one of the closest daylilies to true pink. Other excellent forms include H.'Little Wine Cup', which has burgundy red blooms with a yellow throat; H.'Cream Drop', with its small, creamy yellow flowers; H. 'Buzz Bomb', which is a deep, velvety red, and H. 'Chartreuse Magic', which produces canary yellow and green flowers.

Hemerocallis 'Crimson Pirate'

Hemerocallis 'Buzz Bomb'

There are only a handful of double-flowered varieties, and they do not generally add much to the range. Arguably the best double Hemerocallis is *H. fulva* 'Flore Pleno', with its reddish orange coloured flowers.

Daylilies can be planted at any time from mid-autumn until mid-spring. The soil should be enriched, and when fully established some general fertilizer and mulching in spring will help produce fine flowers. The preferred site for most Hemerocallis would be to plant them in full sun or light shade (heavy shade can often depress flower production). Most soils are tolerated, but these plants perform best in fairly rich, loamy soil.

Maintenance is fairly easy. Cut back any dead flowerstalks to the base, as soon as the last flowers on them have faded.

To propagate, lift and divide overgrown plants in autumn or spring; or sow seed in a cold frame or greenhouse in autumn or spring.

KEY FACTS

Flowers red, purple, pink, yellow; late spring to mid-autumn
Plant mid-autumn to mid-spring
Site full sun/light shade
Min Temp -20°C
Height 45–120cm
Spread 60–90cm

HIPPURIS VULGARIS

Mare's tail

Although there is a similarity in habit to the rampant weed horsetail (*Equisetum vulgare*), this plant bears no relation to that weed. *Hippuris vulgaris* is an attractive perennial, found growing naturally in waterways throughout mainland Europe. Although tiny green flowers appear in summer, the strength of the plants comes with its foliage. Numerous short, narrow, deciduous needle-like leaves come in spirals up the stalks. The underwater portions of the stems carry thinner and more flimsy leaves.

Hippuris vulgaris

KEY FACTS
Flowers insignificant and green; early to late summer
Plant early–late spring
Site full sun or shade
Min Temp -20°C
Height 40cm
Spread 45cm

CARE: Hippuris has a preferred water depth of around 60cm (24in), but will grow adequately in depths considerably less or more. Propagation is by division any time during spring.

HOSTA

Plantain lily

Hostas are principally grown for their large, graceful leaves. There are more than 70 species and hundreds of modern varieties. There are few hardy herbaceous plants that can match the variety, diversity of form, texture and leaf colourings as the hosta. These are fast-spreading, clump-forming plants that enhance any waterside environment.

Hostas have always been thought of as plants for the damp, shadier parts of the garden, but most gardeners now recognize them as much more versatile plants, often tolerating sunny, dry spots too.

The leaves vary in size from those which are just a few centimetres (couple of inches) long, to the largest

which are dinner plate-sized. Just as the sizes vary, so do the textures of the leaves, from very smooth, through to shiny, dull, matt and even corrugated. Add to these variables the bewildering array of leaf colours and variegations, and one can see why they are among

Hosta sieboldiana

some of our most popular plants.

In summer they produce long stems of small, nodding, lily-like flowers in shades of lilac, mauve and purple, as well as a few which are pure white. Some selections are even fragrant.

Probably the most popular species of hosta is *Hosta fortunei*, and one of the most attractive forms is *H. fortunei* var. *albopicta*. It has bright yellow leaves distinctively edged with green in spring, which change to all-over green

Top *Hosta fortunei* var. *aureomarginata, with its flower spikes,* below.

as they age. Meanwhile, *H. fortunei* var. *aureomarginata* (syn. *H.* 'Fortunei Aureomarginata') has leaves of a rich dark green with a yellow border, and *H. fortunei* var. *hyacinthina* has slightly shiny, small green leaves with long points.

H. crispula is a great favourite, with striking white-margined broad, pointed dark green leaves. It also

Hosta fortunei

offers stems of lilac-purple flowers in mid-summer. *H. decorata* has bold ribbed leaves with cream margins; it also produces pale purple flowers. *H. elata* is among the earliest of hostas to flower, producing pale lilac blooms in the early summer, held aloft pale green matt leaves with wavy edges.

Wavy edged foliage is a characteristic of the varieties of *H. undulata*. One of the earliest varieties is *H. undulata* var. *albomarginata,* with a strong creamy-white edge to the leaves.

There are a growing number of nurseries that specialize in hostas, so contact them for advice on which of the several hundred cultivars and hybrid hostas to choose from.

Plant hostas in spring, preferably in full sun or dappled shade. Cut or pull away tattered foliage once it starts to look bad.

Division of hosta clumps during the autumn or spring is the best way to propagate

KEY FACTS

Flowers lilac, mauve, white; late spring/summer

Plant early–mid-spring/mid- to late autumn

Site shade to full sun

Min Temp -20˚C

Height 30–120cm

Spread 30–150cm

this plant. If you delay carrying this out until the new growths have started to appear in spring, it is possible to prise the clumps away from the main crown of the plant without having to lift the complete thing.

Hosta undulata var. *univittata*

The biggest problem any gardener is likely to have is the damage caused by slugs and snails. Frequent 'baiting' around the plants with proprietary poison-based pellets, gels or tapes is commonplace.

Gardeners who prefer the organic approach often use half grapefruits or small sunken cups containing beer. Both will attract the pests, at which point you can gather them up and dispose of them however you see fit. This should be carried out from mid-spring onwards. Failure to do this will result in badly chewed leaves which can soon become an eyesore.

CARE: Mulch in spring or autumn, and give a handful of general fertilizer for each plant in spring. Cut back any dead flower stalks as soon as they have faded.

HOTTONIA

Water violet

If you want a floating water plant with attractive flowers held well above the surface of the water, and which doubles as an oxygenator, then choose the water violet. The flowers, when combined with leaves that protrude out of the water, give this plant the appearance of a marginal. In shallow water Hottonia will root in mud at the bottom, but in deeper water they will rest below the surface before they throw up the flower spikes. Still water is preferred, so avoid ponds that are fed by cascades or have fountains. Hottonia is suitable for a small pond, as well as a larger wildlife one.

Hottonia palustris

KEY FACTS
Flowers white, pale lilac; early to mid-summer
Plant early–late spring
Site full sun or medium shade
Min Temp -20˚C
Height 30–40cm
Spread 100cm

CARE: Thin out excessive growth during summer. In autumn, plants die down and pass the winter as dormant buds. These sink to the bottom, rise and produce new growth in spring.

HOUTTUYNIA CORDATA

Orange peel plant

This is a vigorous, semi-evergreen plant for the water's edge or bog garden. It makes attractive ground cover and can become invasive unless confined. Plant directly into the soil at the edge of the pond or in baskets to restrain root spread. Planting should be into

Houttuynia cordata

wet soil or directly into shallow water, no deeper than 10cm (4in). In early summer small, white, four-petalled flowers appear on short stalks above the leaves. The leaves are more interesting than the flowers and come in shades of pink, yellow, green, cream and white.

CARE: Remove dead or fading foliage and tidy up in the autumn. To protect soil-grown plants from frost, mulch with compost in the autumn.

KEY FACTS

Flowers white; early to mid-summer

Plant early–late spring

Site full sun/shade, but best in partial shade

Min Temp -20˚C

Height 30cm

Spread 45cm

HYDROCHARIS MORSUS-RANAE

Frogbit

This attractive floating plant looks similar to a tiny waterlily. The leaves are small, deciduous, rounded or heart-shaped, and are green-bronze in colour. The leaves are both floating and raised above the water surface. Drop young frogbits in the water during spring. They will perform at their best in a still pond. Thin out established plants several times a year. Frogbit is useful as a surface cover plant for wildlife ponds. It survives the winter as dormant buds, which fall to the bottom of the pond. Watch out for attacks from water snails.

Hydrochari morsus-ranae

KEY FACTS

Flowers white with yellow centre; mid- to late summer
Plant early–late spring
Site full sun/light shade
Min Temp -20˚C
Height 5cm
Spread 100+cm

CARE: Pond water must not be allowed to freeze at the bottom because this is where the overwintering buds are protected from the severe cold as they hibernate.

IRIS FULVA

This is a pale copper-red iris, a fairly unusual colour for a water iris. Its natural habitats are the warm, wetlands of south Louisiana in the USA, hence it is classified by specialists to be in a small group called the Louisiana Irises (see also *Iris x fulvala*).

All water irises have many forms of flowers: single flowers have three petals and three upright standards (almost petals). The petals have what is known as a signal flash in the centre near the stem, and this can be of a variety of colours. Double flowers have six petals, where the standards have actually become petals.

There are many Louisiana hybrids still being bred, particularly in North America, and these are something to look forward to. They have so far produced some

Iris fulva 'Marvell Gold'

Iris fulva 'Dwarf Terracotta'

stunning results, with flowers of pale pink, white, red, yellow, blue and purple, some with ruffled edges and others so double that they look more like a camellia than an iris.

Iris fulva produces lush green foliage, appearing early in the spring, giving the pond a luxuriant, green effect before much of the other garden foliage has emerged.

KEY FACTS

Flowers copper, gold; late spring to mid-summer
Plant mid-spring to mid-summer
Site still pond, full sun
Min Temp -5°C
Height 45–80cm
Spread 100+cm

CARE: Remove dead leaves and deadhead faded flowers before seeds are set (unless you are collecting seed), otherwise flowering may be reduced the following year.

IRIS LAEVIGATA

*Japanese water iris
or Rabbit ear iris*

This is arguably the most important iris for growing in water. The three-petalled blooms of straight *Iris laevigata* are about 12.5cm (5in) across. The first flowers open in early summer and are a clear blue-violet with a yellow line down each petal. Among the best varieties is 'Alba', with its pure white, single blooms; 'Mottled Beauty' has white flowers with pale mauve mottling at the base. One of the most popular cultivars is the double flowered 'Colchesterensis'.

KEY FACTS

Flowers blue, violet, white; early summer
Plant early–late spring
Site still pond, full sun or light shade
Min Temp -5°C
Height 60–90cm
Spread 100+cm

CARE: If plants are enjoying life in the right conditions, a second flush of flowers may appear in late summer or early autumn.

Iris laevigata

IRIS PSEUDACORUS

Yellow flag iris

The yellow flag iris is the most common of water irises, and roots of it will grow vigorously. It will, within reason, grow in any depth of water. This iris can be extremely prolific, spreading rapidly across the pond.

It is possible to roughly chop up small sections with leaves and weigh them down in 37cm (15in) of water, and for the plant to grow away with great success.

Regardless of its vigour, it is worth a place in the water garden. The species produces large golden flowers and brown signal flashes. It needs a lot of room in which to grow, so should only be planted into a medium to large pond. There are a number of excellent varieties. One of the most popular is 'Flore Pleno': this is a hose-in-hose iris, which means that the flower is constructed from many blooms, each one growing inside another.

Iris pseudacorus

More diminutive are 'Golden Queen', a completely golden iris with no brown signal flashes, and *Iris pseudacorus* var. *bastardii*, a cream variety with pale brown signals. You could try 'Ecru', an almost white flower with dark brown signals. 'Alba' is a pale creamy white form with brown signals, and 'Roy Davidson' has golden yellow flowers, heavily veined with brown down the whole of the petal.

'Variegata' has golden flowers with deep yellow and green variegated leaves. Finally, there is a vigorous cultivar with the unlikely name 'Turnipseed'. The flag is extremely strong, able to reach 2m (6ft) high, with golden yellow flowers.

Iris pseudacorus

KEY FACTS
Flowers cream, white, gold; late spring to early summer
Plant early–late spring
Site full sun/light shade
Min Temp -20˚C
Height 150–200cm
Spread 100+cm

CARE: If you have a smallish pond, it would be sensible to divide your clump every couple of years for the best flowering results.

IRIS VERSICOLOR   *American blue flag*

Although known as the American blue flag, it actually has a bright green flag (the green leaf part of the plant) with a profusion of small flowers. Its flower stalks are 45–60cm (18–24in) high, the leaves reaching a little higher still. It comes in various colours, the norm being pale blue, through to darker blue, but there are white forms as well as many named varieties. One of these varieties is 'Kermesina', a deep wine red with golden signals. 'Mysterious Monique' has deep red flowers that almost verge to purple.

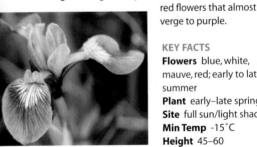

Iris versicolor

KEY FACTS
Flowers blue, white, mauve, red; early to late summer
Plant early–late spring
Site full sun/light shade
Min Temp -15°C
Height 45–60
Spread 100+cm

CARE: Grow plants in containers to prevent spread. Divide every three or four years and pot up offshoots with garden soil. Aphids and iris sawfly can cause problems.

IRIS X FULVALA

As with *Iris fulva*, this is one of the Louisiana irises which are naturally distributed in the warm and wetlands of the southern USA. In appearance, however, this iris is totally different. It is a much showier iris, with large, rich red-purple flowers and golden signals.

Similar characteristics are that it produces lush green foliage early in the spring, before many other types of garden plants have come into leaf. It is a robust, rhizomatous iris.

Iris x fulvala plants prefer a still pond or waterway in full sun, but they will generally perform well in light shade.

Newly bought containerized plants will be growing in a suitable soil, but if you are replanting, use good, clean garden soil from a part of the garden that has not recently been dressed with fertilizer. Remove twigs, weeds, old leaves or anything likely to decay and foul the water.

Plant between early spring and late spring.

Iris x fulvala

Little general care is required once plants are established. Remove any dead or scrappy leaves when seen.

This iris will benefit from lifting and dividing every three or four years during mid- to late spring. Use garden soil to pot up the offshoots into new aquatic pots. To prevent fish from disturbing the soil, and small soil particles floating away, place gravel or small stones over the surface.

Aphids, caterpillars and earwigs are the main pests, while there are several viruses that can affect flowering and leaf production. Because of the risk of chemical run-off into the pondwater, insecticide controls are not possible, so the pests should simply be washed off with a jet of water from a hosepipe, and allowed to sink or swim! However, none of these problems is generally considered to be life-threatening.

This iris will grow equally well in a bog garden or pond.

CARE: Deadhead faded flowers before seeds are set (unless you want to collect the seed), otherwise flowering may be reduced the following year.

KEY FACTS
Flowers violet, mauve; early to mid-summer
Plant early–late spring
Site still pond in full sun or light shade
Min Temp -15˚C
Height 45cm
Spread 100+cm

LEUCOJUM

Snowflake

Easily confused with a snowdrop, *Leucojum vernum* – the spring snowflake – is a larger plant. Blooms are bell-shaped and nodding. Leaves are strap-like, rich green and grow in tufts. *L. aestivum* is the summer snowflake and taller than its spring cousin at 60cm (2ft); the best form is 'Gravetye Giant'. Avoid growing the autumn snowflake (*L. autumnale*) in the bog garden, as it prefers drier conditions. Plant bulbs 7.5cm (3in) deep and 10cm (4in) apart in groups of five or more for best effect.

Leucojum vernum

KEY FACTS

Flowers white with green/yellow spots; late winter to mid-spring
Plant early–mid autumn
Site full sun/light shade
Min Temp -15°C
Height 20–60cm
Spread 10–20cm

CARE: Mulch over the bulb area in autumn and give a general fertilizer in spring. Remove the faded blooms and divide overcrowded clumps after four or five years.

LOBELIA

Cardinal flower

Aquatic lobelias are different to the annual lobelias, but mainly they are hardier, taller and not blue! Although many gardeners are tempted to grow them in ordinary garden soil, they only perform at their best with their roots under water. The hybrid of *Lobelia cardinalis*, 'Queen Victoria', is stunning, with carmine flowers and blood-red leaves. Three closely related species are *L. fulgens*, *L. dortmanna* and *L. siphillitica*. Plant aquatic lobelias in water 5–15cm (2–6in) deep, but most perform well in a moist bog garden.

Lobelia cardinalis

KEY FACTS
Flowers red, violet, mauve; early summer to early autumn
Plant early–late spring
Site full sun/light shade
Min Temp -10˚C
Height 90–100cm
Spread 30–40cm

CARE: Cut down all top growth in autumn and, if they are growing in a bog garden, cover the crowns with straw or bracken to protect them from the worst of the frosts.

LYCHNIS

Ragged robin

An attractive flower of natural marshes and damp places, Lychnis is not one of the more spectacular of bog plants, yet it is always welcome – and lovely in a wild waterside context. Large blooms are carried on long, reddish stalks. The leaves are narrow and

Lychnis chalcedonica

sparse, and grow in thin clumps. The white-flowered *Lychnis flos-cuculi* var. *albiflora* is worth making room for. The best related plant for a bog garden is *L. chalcedonica,* also known as the Maltese cross, the Jerusalem cross or catchfly. The best garden position for Lychnis is in any moist (or even wet) soil.

CARE: Space them 15cm (6in) apart, in small groups. Cut down all growth in autumn, but otherwise they are relatively undemanding.

KEY FACTS

Flowers red, pink, white; late spring to mid-summer
Plant early–late spring
Site full sun/light shade
Min Temp -20˚C
Height 45–90cm
Spread 30cm

LYSICHITON

Skunk cabbage

Lysichiton americanus

KEY FACTS

Flowers yellow, creamy-white; mid- to late spring
Plant mid-autumn–early spring
Site partial shade/full sun
Min Temp -15°C
Height 75–90cm
Spread 60cm

Lysichiton is a real star of the bog garden, despite its unpleasant aroma close up. It really pays to grow this next to water, where the reflection of its spathes can add to the magnificence. The leaves, which appear in late spring, are long, rounded and a fresh yellow-green. Plants may prove a little slow to flower, but they are well worth persevering with. The best position is in partial shade, although it likes growing in full sun almost as much. To propagate, sow fresh seed in moist soil during late spring or early summer.

CARE: An undemanding plant, but it pays to provide twice-yearly mulches in spring and autumn. Feed with a general fertilizer in spring. Do not disturb the plants once established.

LYTHRUM

Purple loosestrife

An impressive plant, especially when a large group is in full bloom. *Lythrum salicaria* (the form that is best for wildlife ponds) attracts bees, several types of butterflies and other insects. Lythrum is an adaptable plant that will grow in anything from dry soil to a position where its roots are permanently in water. The two species that offer the best potential for bog gardens are *L. salicaria* and *L. virgatum*. The former is the natural loosestrife found in the wild. *L. virgatum* is more suitable for the small bog garden as its hybrids are shorter in height.

Lythrum salicaria

CARE: Self-sown seedlings can be difficult to weed out, so cut off the flowerheads if you do not want the plants to spread. Lightly mulch in spring.

KEY FACTS

Flowers pink, purple, orange; early to late summer
Plant early–late spring
Site moist soil in full sun
Min Temp -20°C
Height 90–200cm
Spread 30cm

MATTEUCCIA

This plant will spread almost indefinitely if it is happy with its soil and surrounding environment. *Matteuccia struthiopteris* is a deciduous fern, dying back completely in late autumn. In spring you cannot fail to be impressed by the masses of new, infertile leaves that are produced, unfurling from a basal rosette around central, dark brown permanent fertile fronds.

Matteuccia struthiopteris

M. orientalis produces lance-shaped fronds, initially green but soon turning brown. Propagation is not usually an issue with Matteuccia, as the fern has a natural willingness to spread.

CARE: Remove dead fronds in spring so they do not interfere with the current season's growth. Mulch the area around the roots with compost each spring.

KEY FACTS
Foliage lime-green, brown fronds
Plant early–late spring
Site moist, well mulched soil in light shade
Min Temp -20˚C
Height 90–150cm
Spread 100+cm

MENTHA AQUATICA

Water ...

The flowers are characteristic of most mints: tiny and fragrant, in tight round clusters at the ends of shoots. Before flowering, leaf and stem growth can be rapid, and you may need to control them. The deciduous, small, oval, woolly or hairy leaves are dark green turning reddish purple in bright sun. Like other mints, they are heavily scented when crushed. Propagation can be carried out easily in any of three ways: by dividing up clumps, sowing seed in spring, or by taking easy-to-root stem cuttings in the spring or summer.

KEY FACTS

Flowers mauve, lilac-blue; mid-summer to early autumn
Plant early–late spring
Site full sun/light shade
Min Temp -20°C
Height 5–45cm
Spread 30–75cm

Menta aquatica

CARE: Plant in groups of three or four for impact. If planted in baskets, it is much easier to keep in check. Cut down all growth in the autumn. Divide clumps every other year.

MENYANTHES TRIFOLIATA   *Bog bean*
or Marsh trefoil

The roots of this plant grow perfectly well in the muddy
soil at the sides of the pond, and will just as happily
creep out into deeper water to grow as a true aquatic.
As well as its star-shaped flowers, the reddish flower
buds are attractive in their own right. The aerial rooted
stems are ideal for propagation – remove them from
the plant, pot them horizontally in a heavy loam, then
submerge the pot. Or, propagate by dividing larger
clumps every four or five years. Do this in spring, cutting
the creeping rhizomes into several rooted sections.

Menyanthes trifoliata

KEY FACTS
Flowers white, pink; mid-
spring to early summer
Plant mid- to late autumn
or early to late spring
Site full sun/light shade
Min Temp -20˚C
Height 10cm
Spread 100+cm

CARE: This plant grows best in a soil that is slightly acid,
and a depth of water as much as 25cm (10in) will not harm
it. Cut down dead stems in autumn.

MILIUM EFFUSUM
Golden wood millet or Bowles' golden grass

The golden form of this plant, 'Aureum', is an excellent lightener of semi-shaded places in the garden, and is a real gem of spring and early summer. Every above-ground part of the plant is bright yellow: the broad, soft, somewhat floppy leaves, the flowering stems, and the open panicles of tiny spikelets on hair-fine branches in early summer. It has a slightly greener appearance as the season progresses, or if it is grown in too much shade. Although this plant can fade after three or four years, when it is well suited to its conditions it will self-seed happily.

KEY FACTS
Flowers yellow, browny-yellow; early to mid-summer
Plant early–late spring
Site light shade
Min Temp -20°C
Height 30–35cm
Spread 45–50cm

CARE: Enrich the soil by mulching in spring and autumn; feed in spring with a general fertilizer. Allow leaves to die down naturally after flowering.

Milium effusum 'Aureum'

MIMULUS

Water musk, Yellow musk or Monkey flower

Several musk flowers make excellent plants for pond edges and margins, but they do need room to grow (being fairly invasive and with their propensity to self-seed), so larger water gardens make the best homes.

Depending on the species and cultivar, yellow, orange, red or lavender-blue flowers are carried on tall spikes. Close-up, the blooms have pronounced lips, rather like snapdragons. The leaves are small, rounded, mid-green and deciduous.

The water musk (*Mimulus luteus*) produces yellow blooms with red blotches during mid-summer. The cardinal flower (*M. cardinalis*, and not to be confused with the other cardinal flower, *Lobelia cardinalis*) has attractive downy leaves and bright red, almost scarlet flowers throughout summer. The great purple monkey flower (*M. lewisii*) carries pink to wine purple coloured flowers from early summer to mid-autumn, and the lavender musk (*M. ringens*), not surprisingly, carries pale lavender coloured flowers.

Mimulus lewisii

The blooms of the monkey musk (*M. moschatus*) are entirely yellow. In past centuries, this was one of the most richly perfumed garden flowers. Then, inexplicably, around the year 1914, all strains of this plant across the world lost much of their fragrance – and have never regained it.

Mimulus moschatus

Musks, most of which hail from North America, grow best in full sun in water 0–8cm (0–3in) deep – but 8–15cm (3–6in) deep in the case of *M. ringens*. Set out young plants, or transplant self-sown seedlings, in spring. Cut back dead or dying stems in the autumn.

KEY FACTS
Flowers red, yellow, mauve; early summer to early autumn
Plant early–late spring
Site full sun
Min Temp -20°C
Height 15–90cm
Spread 30–50+cm

CARE: To propagate, divide overcrowded plants every two or three years in spring. Take softwood cuttings in summer. Seed of some forms, such as *M. ringens*, can be sown in spring.

MYOSOTIS SCORPIOIDES

Water forget-me-not

Myosotis scorpioides

This plant grows easily in most situations and is very reliable. Its creeping rhizomes are not invasive; they will trail into the water, making it ideal for masking pond edges. It is useful for underplanting irises and other tall aquatics. Deciduous, small, oval, bright green leaves covered in short hairs are carried on long trailing stems. Plant in moist soil close to the water's edge; a depth of soil 0–15cm (0–6in) is ideal. It will equally tolerate full sun and heavy shade; some say this plant is the most shade-tolerant of all flowering aquatics.

KEY FACTS

Flowers blue, white, pink; mid-spring to mid-summer
Plant mid- to late autumn
Site shade to full sun
Min Temp -20˚C
Height 30cm
Spread 60cm

CARE: A single plant will spread to 60cm (2ft) in a year; the stems are much longer, but trail down. Cut down old, dead growth in autumn.

MYRIOPHYLLUM

Milfoil

Milfoils are loved by fish as a spawning ground and provide an excellent refuge for young fish, in addition to oxygenating the pond. The most common milfoil found in outdoor ponds is *Myriophyllum aquaticum*. This has very dense, ferny foliage that emerges from the water. Grow in baskets of loamy soil, at a depth of 1m (3ft). The plant tends to die back in winter to dormant crowns that rest well beneath the surface of the water, or it is liable to become damaged by frosts. These crowns then re-emerge below the surface in spring.

Myriophyllum aquaticum

KEY FACTS

Flowers insignificant and white; early to late spring
Plant throughout spring and summer
Site loamy soil, full sun
Min Temp 4°C
Height 30cm
Spread 50+cm

CARE: Self-rooting stems are often produced, and these may be separated and replanted. Otherwise, take stem cuttings in spring or summer to propagate.

NELUMBO

Lotus blossom

Even if you live in a cooler climate, as long as you have a pond you can grow lotuses. However, unless you live in areas where these plants grow well outdoors all year round, either in gardens or naturally in waterways, you will have to search for them from specialist dealers. The plants will reward you, as long as you also expend a little effort in protecting them from frosts.

There are two species, the hardiest of which is the north American chinkapin (*Nelumbo lutea*). It is the smaller of the two, growing to 2m (6ft) in height, with large and showy yellow blossoms. Although not often grown outside in more cooler regions, it is a reasonably hardy plant and should produce plenty of typical plate-like foliage, if not many flowers.

The Asian sacred lotus (*N. nucifera*) is a giant of a plant in its original form, but one which has given us a

range of dwarf cultivars. Try the white, pink-edged 'Chawan Basu' or the carmine-pink 'Pekinensis Rubra'. Instead of growing them in the pool try them in a large

Nelumbo nucifera

tub or container at the
waterside.

Most lotuses open their
flowers early in the day –
often before dawn – and
will produce a second
flush of flowers during
late summer or even
early autumn, as long as
there has been a fairly
hot summer.

Nelumbo nucifera

KEY FACTS

Flowers white, pink,
yellow; early to mid-
summer, early autumn
Plant early–late spring
Site full sun, warm pond
Min Temp 1°C
Height 120–200cm
Spread 100cm

CARE: When container grown, Nelumbo can be easily
moved indoors during the autumn for overwintering in
a frost-free place.

NUPHAR

Yellow pond lily, Brandy bottle or Spatterdock

Nuphar, although related to the Nymphaeas, is vigorous and therefore invasive. It is suited to large, deep ponds or lakes. *Nuphar lutea* is often referred to as brandy bottle, owing both to the shape of the flowers and their 'alcoholic' scent. Leaves come in two different forms: under the water they are translucent, thin and feathery, while those on the water are rounded, heart-shaped and up to 30cm (12in) across. *N. japonica* var. *variegata* and *N. pumila variegata* are much smaller varieties.

Nuphar lutea

KEY FACTS
Flowers yellow; early to late summer
Plant early–late spring
Site large pond in full sun or partial shade
Min Temp -20°C
Height 10–15cm
Spread 200+cm

CARE: During spring, plant rhizomes or young plants into baskets. Remove dead foliage or flowers and wash off any aphids that might be seen. Otherwise, easy to care for.

NYMPHAEA

Waterlilies

Generally, native species of Nymphaea are not the best for most ponds, because they are not as ornamental and do not perform as reliably as the named cultivars. All hardy Nymphaea are day-flowerers, but on dark, cloudy days they may not open at all. Unless the plants are overcrowded, flowers usually rest on the water surface. They come in a wide range of colours, from the purest of whites to the darkest of reds.

PYGMY WATERLILIES

Pygmy waterlilies are excellent for sinks, troughs or ponds where the water is no deeper than 30cm (12in). Most of these will grow well in just 10cm (4in) of water or even in the deeper marginal shelves of a larger pond.

There are two notes of caution when it comes to growing these small varieties. The first is the likelihood of the plants freezing in winter: despite being hardy, the plants grow in very shallow water, which in the harshest of winters can freeze solid. Provide

Nymphaea 'Pygmaea Alba'

the plants with sufficient depth to ensure that the rhizomes remain unfrozen during the coldest spells. If this is not possible, protect them by lifting the plants in mid-autumn and keeping them in water in a frost-free place until planting time again.

The second warning concerns the fact that these small waterlilies are perfect for growing in contained water features, such as a barrel, tub or sink. There is a temptation, however, for many of us to fit a small ornamental fountain or a regular drip-drip feature of some kind. All waterlilies, of whatever size, dislike moving water around their leaves and stems, which suppresses flowering, and this problem can be exacerbated in a container.

Nymphaea 'Pygmaea Alba' (also sold as *N. tetragona*) has white, single blooms with golden yellow stamens. The leaves are deep green, dark red beneath, and tiny. It is the only waterlily that can be grown in an aquarium with any degree of success. 'Pygmaea Rubra', meanwhile, has blood red single flowers with orange stamens. The purplish-green leaves have reddish undersides. Slightly larger is 'Pygmaea Rubis', with single, wine red flowers and yellow stamens.

CARE: Site newly bought containerized waterlilies straight away. Divide every three or four years during mid- to late spring. Watch out for aphids, waterlily beetle and leaf miners.

SMALL WATERLILIES

These waterlilies are ideal for the smaller pond or large container water features, with a water depth of 10–30cm (4–12in). They generally have a spread of around 30–60cm (1–2ft).

Nymphaea 'Froebelii'

Known as a chameleon or changeable waterlily, *N.* 'Aurora' produces semi-double flowers of mid-yellow, gradually changing through orange to red. This can happen over several days, so a number of different colours may be seen at the same time, adding to its appeal. Its stamens are yellow, and it has mid-green leaves with attractive mottled and marbled patterns. It is best in a depth of 30–45cm (12–18in) and can spread to 12–24in (30–60cm). 'Aurora' is ideal for a tub garden container.

The fragrant blooms of 'Paul Hariot' are semi-double yellow, turning reddish-orange with yellow stamens. The mid-green leaves have a purplish flecking.

'Froebelii' is vivid red, single, with yellow stamens and mid-green leaves. 'Graziella' is coppery-red, single, with orange stamens and pale green leaves with purple flecking. 'Maurice Laydeker' is a single, deep red with white flecks on the outer petals, and yellow stamens.

A very popular and old variety is 'Johann Pring', which produces deep pink, single flowers, with stamens in two rings – the inner ones are pale orange, and the outer ones deep pink.

COMPACT WATERLILIES

These are ideal for small ponds or large contained water features, with a water depth of 30–60cm (12–24in). They have a spread of 60–100cm (2–3ft).

There are a number of yellows, including 'Odorata Sulphurea Grandiflora' (yellow, semi-double, yellow stamens, mid-green leaves with brown markings); 'Sioux' (yellow, turning orange then rich red, semi-double, yellow stamens, greenish bronze leaves with brown mottling); and 'Solfatare' (yellow, turning orange-yellow and then red, single, yellow stamens, dark green leaves with purple blotches and spots).

Nymphaea 'Albatross'

One of the most widely seen compact waterlilies is 'James Brydon', crimson, semi-double to double, fragrant, red stamens with gold tips, dark purple-green leaves with maroon flecks.

In the 'compact' category there are only a few white forms, and the best is generally regarded to be 'Albatross'. Its pure white, single, flowers hold golden stamens, and the leaves are purplish, gradually turning deep green.

LARGE WATERLILIES

Perhaps the most dramatic of all waterlilies are the larger cultivars, which are more suited, by definition, to larger ponds – or even lakes. These require a planting depth of 45–80cm (18–32in), and produce a spread of leaves, when established, of up to 2.4m (8ft). Because these plants are usually sited in ponds some distance from the edges, maintaining them can sometimes be a problem. Wading in to the pond, or reaching out with makeshift cutting tools (such as a razor blade attached to a bamboo cane), are often the only options available.

N. 'Gladstoneana' is a true giant of a waterlily: double, white, fragrant

Nymphaea 'Gladstoneana'

flowers hold golden-yellow stamens. Another variety, 'Mrs Richmond', is an equally impressive large waterlily, with double pale pink flowers turning to red, and yellow stamens.

TROPICAL WATERLILIES

Waterlilies from tropical climates have an entirely different appeal to the hardy form discussed above. Many are highly fragrant and have been used in the making of perfumes. They are important enough to deserve a mention, but they are really only suitable for growing under conservatory conditions, or outside in hot, humid countries.

They tend to be more floriferous than the hardy types, and the most common flower colour is blue. They can also be very vigorous, often reaching 2.4m (8ft) in a season. Planting should only take place when the water has reached a temperature of 21°C (70°F).

Nymphaea 'Perry's Pink'

KEY FACTS
Flowers multi-coloured; early summer to early autumn
Plant early–late spring
Site still pond in full sun
Min Temp -20°C
Height 15–20cm
Spread 45–240cm

NYMPHOIDES PELTATA

Water fringe

Curiously, the yellow blooms do not look like waterlilies. Each flower is 5cm (2in) across, and the petals have frilled edges. Sadly, blooms only last one day, but a large area will produce so many flowers that there will always be a few open on each day of the flowering season. The ideal water depth is 45cm (18in). Although the straight species is most commonly seen, *Nymphoides peltata* 'Bennettii' is becoming more widely available. It produces slightly larger flowers than the species, but lacks some of the attractive leaf mottling.

Nymphoides peltata **'Bennettii'**

CARE: Unless you have a large pond, contain them within planting baskets. It is advisable to lift plants out of the pond and divide them every spring.

KEY FACTS

Flowers yellow; mid-summer to early autumn
Plant early–late spring
Site large pond in full sun or light shade
Min Temp -20˚C
Height 10cm
Spread 100+cm

OSMUNDA

Regal fern

Osmunda claytoniana

Osmunda is a highly desirable plant for large bog gardens, and is very vigorous and spreading. *Osmunda regalis* 'Purpurascens' has purple-green stems and fronds, and markedly pink-brown young shoots. 'Cristata', the crested royal fern, is smaller, with attractively tasselled foliage. *O. claytoniana,* the interrupted fern, derives its common name from the spores that are borne around the stalk in a part of the frond that is devoid of leaflets. Leaflets above and below this spore area develop normally, giving the frond the appearance of having been interrupted.

KEY FACTS

Foliage lime green, copper-tinted in spring, yellow-bronze in autumn
Plant early–late spring
Site full sun/light shade
Min Temp -20˚C
Height 90–210cm
Spread 90–180cm

CARE: The ideal soil is moist and acid. Mulch with garden compost after planting, and annually every spring, feeding with a general fertilizer.

PELTANDRA

Arrow arum

The leaves are bright green, shiny, strongly veined and arrow-shaped. Sometimes the undersides of the leaves take on a chestnut hue. When grown in deeper water, they tend to be evergreen. Set plants out, around 30cm (12in) apart, during spring. The ideal water depth is 0–25cm (0–10in). It is best to plant directly into the soil, as Peltandra does not take kindly to container growing. To propagate, divide the creeping rhizomes in spring. Sometimes the white arrow arum (*Peltandra sagittifolia* or *P. alba*) has flowers of a purer white, with red autumn berries. *P. virginica* often turns evergreen in deep water.

Peltandra sagittifolia

KEY FACTS
Flowers greenish-white with white spathe; early to mid-summer
Plant early–late spring
Site full sun/light shade
Min Temp -15˚C
Height 60cm
Spread 45cm

CARE: Remove any faded foliage in late autumn. In winter, protect plants not under water by packing straw or bracken around the crowns.

PENNISETUM

Fountain grass

Grasses in the Pennisetum genus generally feature bristly flowers resembling bottle brushes or hairy caterpillars. In cool, dull summers there may not be such a good show of flowers, which is why several cultivars were introduced. *Pennisetum alopecuroides* 'Woodside' is probably the best, and shorter than the species. 'Weserbergland' has a similar smaller stature, but with greeny white flowers. 'Cassian' has notable autumn colouring. 'Little Bunny' is small at 30cm (12in) when in flower, while 'Hameln' is slightly larger, growing to 45cm (18in).

Pennisetum alopecuroides

KEY FACTS
Flowers browny-pink; mid-summer to early autumn
Plant early–late spring
Site moist soil in full sun
Min Temp -15°C
Height 30–90cm
Spread 45–75cm

CARE: Give some protection from the worst of the winter cold. Propagate by division. Lift and divide plants during spring, every three or four years.

PHORMIUM TENAX   *New Zealand flax*

This plant makes a valuable addition to the bog garden for the simple fact that it is the only sword-leaved plant that really enjoys a permanently moist soil. Most phormiums are large, clump-forming plants, with the bonus of keeping their leaves all year round. The best forms have variegated foliage, often with red and pink margins; there are also purple leaved forms. The flower spikes tower over the foliage, opening up into angular, red-brown parrot bill-like flowers. The variegated form, *Phormium tenax* 'Variegatum', is less hardy than the straight species.

Phormium tenax

KEY FACTS

Flowers red-brown, parrot bill-like; early to late summer
Plant early–late spring
Site full sun/light shade
Min Temp -15˚C
Height 90–200cm
Spread 120–250cm

CARE: Do not plant the central base too low, as water can collect here. Feed annually in spring and divide only if overcrowded or to propagate.

PHYSOSTEGIA VIRGINIANA *Obedient plant*

The reason for this plant's curious common name is that the flowers are on hinged stalks, allowing them to be moved into a certain position, where they will remain. Spike-forming plants are helpful in breaking up any tendency to uniformity in the bog garden. Physostegia, with its long flowering habit, fill such a need. It is easy to grow and distinctive. They are, however, subjects that thrive in a good, loamy soil – not an inhospitable waterlogged clay.

Physostegia virginiana

KEY FACTS
Flowers pink, purple, white; late summer to mid-autumn
Plant early–late spring
Site bog garden, full sun
Min Temp -20˚C
Height 50–90cm
Spread 30–60cm

CARE: Mulch in spring and autumn; give a balanced general fertilizer in spring. Cut down dead flowerheads once flowering has finished, and remove top growth in late autumn.

PONTEDERIA CORDATA

Although good as a marginal plant, pickerel weed can become invasive, so it is best treated as a deep-water aquatic, where it can be 'controlled' in baskets. For best appearance, several plants should be grown together, so a medium to large pond is recommended; do not grow Pontederia in water barrels, sinks or other containers. The white-flowered form, *Pontederia cordata alba*, is worth growing. *P. cordata* var. *lancifolia* has slimmer leaves and is a slightly taller plant. The ideal water depth is 10–38cm (4–15in).

Pontederia cordata

CARE: Plants survive the winter provided the crowns are below the ice. If grown in soil at the pond edge, protect crowns in winter with a mulch of straw.

KEY FACTS

Flowers white, blue, purple; mid-summer to early autumn
Plant early–late spring
Site moist soil, full sun
Min Temp -20˚C
Height 75–80cm
Spread 45–50cm

PRIMULA

The Primula genus ranks as one of the largest, most variable and widely appreciated of all plant genera. There are forms for growing in containers, on rockeries, in flower beds, in woodland dells and, of course, at the sides of a pond.

Primulas are all much the same in their growing requirements, which is convenient, but also means that if your garden does not conform, it is unlikely that you will be able to succeed with any of them. In essence, they prefer sunny or lightly shaded places, and a fairly rich, organic, slightly acid soil. The following selection is sure to provide colour and interest in the bog garden.

Primula japonica is possibly the best-known of the

Primula denticulata

candelabra primulas, which bear their flowers in rounded clusters, or whorls, at intervals along the main central stem. It has lush leaves and several tiers of red, pink or white flowers opening at stages during early and mid-summer. Four of the best varieties are: 'Alba' (white), 'Apple Blossom' (pink), 'Miller's Crimson' (deep pink) and 'Postford White' (white).

Another striking candelabra is *P. aurantiaca*, with orange or orange-red blooms that appear in late spring and early summer, which is slightly earlier than similar kinds. The flower stems reach 30cm (12in) in height.

Primula beesiana

Other candelabras include *P. beesiana*, with rich, rosy-purple flowers; *P. x bulleesiana*, with a wide range of colours from yellow, orange and pink through to red and purple; and the pale pink or mauve *P. pulverulenta*.

The 'Drumstick' primula, *P. denticulata*, is extremely popular, with its neat, globular pink-purple heads 8cm (3in) across. There are many garden forms, the flower colours of which are generally given away by their varietal names: 'Glenroy Crimson', 'Inshriach Carmine', 'Prichard's Ruby', 'Robinson's Red' and 'Snowball'.

There is little that can beat a patch of *P. florindae* – the Himalayan cowslip. This plant resembles a very tall, shaggy cowslip – in the case of mature plants growing around 80cm (32in) in height – with slightly powdery, sulphur-yellow flowerheads in early summer. A smaller version of the Himalayan cowslip is *P. sikkimensis*, which has its origins in the Chinese marshlands. It has bright yellow flowers in mid-spring.

One of the most stunning of all primulas is *P. vialii* – the orchid primula. It is distinct from the others, with its startling spikes of bright red buds. In early summer, the lowest buds open to mauve or lilac blooms. The top buds are the last to open, giving the whole flowerhead an impressive dual red/lilac combination.

Finally, there is the lovely *P. rosea*. It is one of the earliest, and tiniest, of bog garden primulas. Vivid rosy pink flowers smother the ground-hugging foliage during early spring.

Primula vialii

KEY FACTS

Flowers multi-coloured; early to late summer
Plant early–late spring
Site moist, humus-rich acidic soil in sun
Min Temp -15˚C
Height 15–90cm
Spread 15–60cm

CARE: Keep adequately moist during the summer, but do not allow to become waterlogged. If soil is only damp, provide some shade or shelter.

PULMONARIA

Lungwort

Pulmonarias are often the earliest of bog garden plants to flower and later their leaves provide interesting ground cover. They are useful for underplanting shrubs or trees in a moisture-retentive soil. The leaves are large, rough and often prominently speckled with white, cream or silver hues. Some people have an allergic reaction to the leaves, but this is not generally a serious fault of the plant. The main reason for growing pulmonarias is for the trumpet-shaped flowers, which fade from bright blue to red, and are held on loose heads on slightly arching stems.

Pulmonaria angustifolia

CARE: Mulch in the autumn to provide a rich, organic soil. Remove flowerheads once blooms start to fade or allow the blooms to set seed.

KEY FACTS

Flowers pink, light to dark blue, red, purple; early to late spring
Plant mid- to late autumn
Site partial or full shade
Min Temp -20˚C
Height 30–45cm
Spread 45cm

RANUNCULUS

Spearwort

Ranunculus lingua will happily extend its creeping roots and colonize a large area. It is a marginal with lovely showy flowers. The blooms are large, some 5cm (2in) across, golden yellow and have a sheen to them that glistens in the sun. Long, spear-shaped leaves – hence the common name – are bright green for most of the season, but pinkish when young. *R. aquatilis* is a spreading, invasive species whose flowers and stems are often submerged underwater. Plant marginal ranunculus either directly into the soil or into planting baskets for siting on ledges around the pond margins.

Ranunculus lingua

KEY FACTS
Flowers golden yellow, white; late spring to early autumn
Plant early–late spring
Site full sun/light shade
Min Temp -20°C
Height 20–90cm
Spread 100+cm

CARE: Remove dying or dead leaves and stems in autumn to avoid polluting the water. Divide overgrown clumps, probably every three to four years, in spring.

RHEUM

Ornamental rhubarb

This is one of the most dramatic bog garden plants. The leaves, when combined with its elongated flowerheads, make it an exotic addition to the bog garden. Leaves are deeply lobed and rich green or purple, with a reddish tinge to the undersides. Each leaf can be 90cm (3ft) across when mature. *Rheum palmatum* 'Atrosanguineum' has red spring leaves; *R. palmatum* var. *tanguticum* has leaves that are deep green tinted purple underneath. To propagate, divide crowns in spring; divide plants every four or five years.

Rheum palmatum

KEY FACTS

Flowers red, purple; late spring to early summer
Plant early–late spring
Site moist, rich soil in full sun or light shade
Min Temp -15˚C
Height 90–300cm
Spread 180–250cm

CARE: Cut down faded flowerheads in late autumn; cover the dormant crowns with straw. Do not let them sit in clay or waterlogged soil, as they are prone to rotting.

RODGERSIA

The shining, rich green leaves of *Rodgersia aesculifolia* are evenly suffused reddish bronze, and have an intricate network of veins. Lovers of bold, dramatic, architectural plants will adore this border perennial. This plant is a classic example of the leaves being so much more important than the flowers! *R. pinnata* 'Superba' has deeply divided leaves and white flowers; *R. podophylla* has palm-shaped leaves and cream flowers; and *R. sambucifolia* has leaves like an elder, and white flowers. Mulch in the spring and autumn and fertilize in the spring.

Rodgersia aesculifolia

CARE: Leave flowerheads in place once they are finished as the reddish seedheads come along later in the season. Do not disturb once established.

KEY FACTS

Flowers pink, white; early to late summer
Plant early–late spring
Site bog garden in light shade
Min Temp -15°C
Height 90–120cm
Spread 90cm

SAGITTARIA

Japanese arrowhead

Sagittaria sagittifolia produces large spikes of white flowers with black and red centres. The male flowers are at the tops of the spikes and females below. The form *S. latifolia* is similar but less hardy, while *S. sagittifolia* 'Flore Pleno' produces double flowers. With more than one plant, set out 23cm (9in) apart. Plant tubers or young plants directly into the soil or weigh them down and drop into the water at the pond's edge. To propagate, divide every second or third year in spring, when overcrowded.

KEY FACTS

Flowers white; early to late summer
Plant early–late spring
Site any water garden in full sun
Min Temp -20°C
Height 25–75cm
Spread 45cm

Sagittaria sagittifolia 'Flore Pleno'

CARE: The preferred water depth is 5–30cm (2–12in); the deeper the water, the fewer the flowers. Cut back all growth in the autumn. If practicable, feed the plants in spring.

SCHOENOPLECTUS LACUSTRIS
Club rush

Schoenoplectus lacustris

One of many aquatic rushes growing in damp soil along the edges of streams and rivers. Even more attractive are the variegated forms: *S. lacustris* subsp. *tabernaemontani* 'Albescens' (with white stems and longitudinal green stripes), and *S. l.* subsp. *tabernaemontani* 'Zebrinus' (green stems and horizontal pale cream stripes). These variegated rushes often revert to the all-green form. Remove any that are seen as soon as possible; in shady spots, fading is less pronounced.

KEY FACTS
Flowers green-brown; early summer to early autumn
Plant early–late spring
Site full sun/light shade
Min Temp -15°C
Height 150–180cm
Spread 45cm

CARE: These plants appreciate being fed with a general fertilizer in spring, and respond by producing beautifully marked, lush growth in quantity.

SPARGANIUM ERECTUM

Branched burr reed

Sparganium erectum performs better if sited in deeper water rather than in the shallows or pond margins. If you have a large pool, plant directly into the soil, otherwise into planting baskets. Avoid planting the burr reed in shallow water where it will soon spread and become a menace. Depending on the depth of water – ideally around 30cm (12in) – the leaves may reach up to 1.5m (5ft) after three years. Normally *S. erectum* is the only species to be seen, but it may sometimes be sold under its less correct name *S. ramosum*.

Sparganium erectum

KEY FACTS
Flowers page green; early to late summer
Plant early–late spring
Site a pond in full sun or light shade
Min Temp -20°C
Height 120–150cm
Spread 100+cm

CARE: To propagate, divide plants in spring. Alternatively, sow fresh seeds into mud in submerged pots. Little on-going care, but remove dead stems and leaves in autumn.

STRATIOTES ALOIDES

Water soldier
or *Water aloe*

This intriguing plant is a semi-evergreen perennial, free-floating, and held partly below and partly above the water. Curiously, plants sink and multiply after flowering, and rise again some weeks later, when surplus offsets can be thinned with a net. It is a good choice for wildlife ponds. They prefer alkaline or limestone waters, which is why they do not always transfer successfully from one pond to another. The leaves are dark olive green, narrow and stiff-toothed, arranged in neat, stalkless rosettes. They usually overwinter at the bottom of the pond.

KEY FACTS

Flowers creamy white, pink; early to late summer
Plant early–late spring
Site alkaline water in full sun/light shade
Min Temp -15°C
Height 10cm
Spread 100+cm

CARE: New plants form as small water buds on spreading stems: separating the clumps in spring and summer is the best way to propagate them.

Stratiotes aloides

TRAPA NATANS

Water chestnut

This is the water chestnut used in Chinese cuisine. The edible fruits are large and thorny, but do not eat any as they are poisonous when raw. It is unlike any other pond plant, with rosettes of deciduous, angular, toothed leaves, each carried on an inflated stalk. Because Trapa throws down hair-like roots into the mud, water depth is important. Grow it in a depth of 30–45cm (12–18in) for best results. Although dormant fruits will survive winters in the bottom of the pond, germination may be erratic in cold climates.

Trapa natans

KEY FACTS

Flowers white; early to late summer
Plant early–late spring
Site still pond in full sun or light shade
Min Temp -5˚C
Height 2.5cm
Spread 100+cm

CARE: To plant, drop young plants into the water. To propagate, sow the spiny fruits in the pool mud; they will give rise to a stem from which floating leaves develop.

TROLLIUS

Globe flower

Trollius europaeus

Globe flowers are incredibly hardy and non-invasive. They are best grown in bold drifts, which is how they grow in the wild. At first glance you could be forgiven for confusing trollius with the marsh marigold (*Caltha palustris*), as both are spring-flowering golden-flowered bog garden buttercups. The easiest way to tell them apart is by their leaves; Trollius have leaves that are divided and buttercup-like, while those of Caltha are glossy and rounded.

The original European globe flower (*Trollius europaeus*) has been tampered with by plant breeders over the years, and now there are many garden varieties available. This main species has as much charm as any of its hybrids, especially if you are growing it in a wild garden. The blooms are bright golden yellow and spherical, hence its common name.

Most of the garden varieties have been grouped under the name *T. x cultorum*. 'Alabaster' is a popular hybrid with the palest of cream flowers. 'Commander in Chief' is a tallish form with spectacular glowing

KEY FACTS
Flowers yellow, orange, cream; late spring to mid-summer
Plant early–mid-spring
Site moist, in light shade
Min Temp -20°C
Height 15–90cm
Spread 30–45cm

Trollius chinensis
'Golden Queen'

orange flowers, and the blooms of 'Pritchard's Giant' are orange-yellow.

T. chinensis is a species found in the Far East, and from which the latest hybrid has been raised. 'Golden Queen' is later flowering and slightly taller than most of the others; it will grow up to 90cm (36in).

The Himalayan *T. pumilis* is a dwarf form at just 15cm (6in) in height, and the blooms are yellow-orange with luscious dark red exteriors.

As wet ground can get cold in winter, to establish trollius (as with most bog garden plants), plant them in spring, before the soil warms up. It is best to plant in groups, with 30cm (12in) between plants.

CARE: They do not perform well if exposed to high winds or the full strength of the sun all day long. Mulch in spring, and deadhead regularly to encourage a second flush of flowers.

TYPHA

Reed mace

This is not a plant for the small – or even lined – pond as it possesses a very strong and vigorous system of pointed roots, capable of penetrating most flexible liners! Typha is best suited to large, natural ponds and lakes. Placing an additional layer of liner between the root system and the pond liner will certainly protect the liner, but it is a great deal of effort for a plant that is not, it must honestly be said, the most decorative of marginals! Old foliage should be cut away during late autumn, otherwise it will die and fall into the water, polluting it. Typhas do not require feeding.

KEY FACTS

Flowers brown, poker-shaped; early to late summer
Plant early–late spring
Site full sun/light shade
Min Temp -20˚C
Height 60–200cm
Spread 100+cm

CARE: To propagate, just remove a length of root system that has healthy tips and roots, pot it into a heavy loam or clay soil, and place it in the water.

Typha laxmannii

ZANTEDESCHIA AETHIOPICA
Arum lily or Calla lily

Zantedeschia aethiopica is a highly variable plant, impossible to say with absolute conviction that it is hardy or half-hardy, deciduous or semi-evergreen or whether it is best as a marginal or a bog garden plant. The variety 'Crowborough' is taller and hardier than the species. 'Green Goddess' is also particularly attractive. 'Apple Court Babe' is a miniature, perfect for around a small pool or contained water feature. The chalk white spathes are carried well above the bright green leaves.

Zantedeschia aethiopica

KEY FACTS
Flowers white; early to late summer
Plant early–late spring
Site pond or bog garden in full sun or partial shade
Min Temp -10˚C
Height 30–90cm
Spread 45–60cm

CARE: Grow zantedeschias in water 5–30cm (2–12in) deep. Plant and divide in spring. Flowers produce many seeds, which can be sown the following autumn or spring.

INDEX

Why not develop your green fingers with these other gardening titles from Collins?

From planning & design to
selecting plants and garden
maintenance, the only garden
book you'll ever need.
336pp   £15.99
PB   0 00 719184 7

Get your containers blooming
from the height of summer to
the depths of winter.
160pp   £6.99
PB   0 00 716404 1

Fill your garden with
drama and dimension.
192pp   £4.99
PB   0 00 720124 9

Packed with projects for getting
kids involved in the garden.
128pp   £14.99
HB   0 00 719311 4

To order any of these titles please telephone **0870 787 1732**
For further information about Collins books visit our website:
www.collins.co.uk